Table

Pt1: The Truth About: Informational Slav

- Common Law vs Admiralty vs Statutory Jurisdiction
- Natural Person vs. ARTIFICIAL PERSON
- The UNITED STATES OF AMERICA is a CORPORATION
- "Right to Travel vs. Driver's License"
- Corpus Delicti= "NO INJURY, NO DAMAGE, NO CRIME!!!"
- Police Power
- Due Process
- Conversion of a right into a Crime
- Arizona Senator's Letter to State Officials
- Big "C" -- Little "c"
- "Acts" are NOT Laws!
- Importance of STATUS

Pt2: The Truth About: The Untold History

- The Moors
- The African Slave Trade "Myth"
- Why is this Information Suppressed?
- Who was here before 1492?
- "Free White Persons"
- The Moors Sundry Act of 1790
- The Period of Reconstruction
- Malcolm X found out he was a MOOR
- The One Dollar Bill is a Contract!!!
- The Iroquois (Moorish) Confederacy
- Documents You MUST know

P3: The Truth About: Commerce

- The Wizard of OZ – an allegory...
- Your Birth Certificate is worth $$$$$
- How can this Birth Certificate Bond be Used to Our Advantage?
- Secure Party Creditor
- How to beat Debt Collectors Forever!

(This is not legal advice...this is for informational purposes only)

"Then you will know the truth, and the truth will set you free..."

Imagine a world where babies are born and their names are instantly turned into corporations. Where birth certificates are worth millions. Where colonists took the law of the seas and imposed it onto the land. Corporations were classified as 'Persons' and had the ability to control, imprison and extract money from people. Where for certain groups of people, it was illegal to learn how to read and write or even own property. This isn't an imaginary world...this is the 20th century in the UNITED STATES OF AMERICA...allow me to explain.

The greatest deception of all, is a deception so huge, and so masterfully put together, that when we are faced with the truth, we refuse to believe it because we feel that there is no way that so many of us could have been so deceived for so long. When first reading or hearing the information that you are about to become privy to, it is very easy to become dismissive and skeptical. Actually, I expect you to become dismissive and skeptical because that will be the fuel needed to gain further understanding for yourself on the various topics that will be presented to you. If I wasn't skeptical about many of this information, I would not have dug as deep as I did to find and understand what it was that I was reading for further comprehension. Once I began to study these various topics and the dots began to connect, it changed my life forever!

I wrote this book, not because I wanted to, but because I had to! Not only was I privileged enough to gain access to this body of information, I was able to understand it, and not only was I able to understand it, I was able to break down the complexities and explain the fundamental concepts to others as well. I began attending classes that were being held in Atlanta, Georgia every week in search for more and more knowledge. As time went on I became one of the top students in the class. Not only did I become one of the top students in the class, but the instructor allowed me to begin teaching the class myself because of the extensive knowledge that I had learned and researched about these subjects. Once word got out about this incredible life changing information, the class grew to standing room only with people crammed into the classroom every week, sometimes twice a week. The reason why is because they realized just as you will, that this information is the most important information you will ever learn about yourself. I wrote this book for the purpose of teaching civics to the community, in order to repair the damage that has been done economically, historically, and civically because of a loss of information. This information is not my opinion; it is a gathering of research being presented to you for your interpretation. As you read, I ask you to read with an open mind and to please do your research on anything that you read in this book for further understanding, insight and clarity.

Lesson #1: Informational Slavery
(What you were never told!!)

People's concept of what slavery is in the Western Hemisphere is all wrong. If we don't understand the body of information that is used to govern and control us then we can't understand HOW and WHY governments are run. When learning this information for the first time one begins to wake up. When waking up we tend to mix emotions with realities. This is not to be left to emotions because getting angry or emotional about this is exactly when we get ourselves away from realities.

To begin this story, we have to start with the International bankers who lent the United States the money to fund their conquest of the Western Hemisphere. Once the United States succeeded in Colonizing the Western Hemisphere, the International bankers needed to be repaid for their contributions. Now understand that the only "lawful" money there has ever been is gold and silver. Therefore, on April 5, 1933, then President Franklin Delano Roosevelt, under Executive Order, issued April 5, 1933, declared: "All persons are required to deliver on or before May 1, 1933 all Gold Coin, Gold Bullion, & Gold Certificates now owned by them to a Federal Reserve Bank, branch or agency, or to any member bank of the Federal Reserve System." This meant that all persons had to relinquish their gold and silver (lawful money) to a Federal Reserve Bank.

Because of this, there was no more green dollars backed by gold in circulation, therefore there was no lawful money, causing the U.S. to **go bankrupt**. Needing desperately to create income, the United States schemed a plan to monetize human beings (Natural Persons) and held a *registration* drive, lured mothers to into registering their biological property (babies), not just material property such as cars and houses.

Note: To <u>register</u> something, is to **transfer ownership** because the person who the item is being transferred to now has the title. This is exactly what happens to your kids when you sign the birth certificate, they become a "ward of state" and that's why the State can take your kids whenever they feel like it.

("The primary control and custody of infants is with the government" Tillman V. Roberts. 108 So. 62)

Since the United States went bankrupt under Roosevelt in 1933, from that time on, all new money has to be BORROWED into existence. **All states started issuing serial-numbered, certified "warehouse receipts" for births in order to pledge us as collateral against those loans taken out with the Federal Reserve Bank.** The "Full faith and Credit" of the United States Citizen backs the government's (corporations) debt! In order to catalog its laborers, the United States Corporation needs a system of tracking its chattel and that is through the social security number. It is always required when you are transacting in any monetary capacity. CITIZENS ARE NOTHING MORE THAN HUMAN RESOURCES!!! The movie "The MATRIX" was right!!

The conspiratorial nature of matters is exemplified in comments by one of the major actors in the triumph of the Federal Reserve, Edward Mandell House, who had this to say in a private meeting with President Woodrow Wilson:

"[Very] soon, every American will be required to **register their biological property** (birth certificates) in a national system designed to keep track of the people and that will operate under the ancient system of pledging. By such methodology, we can compel people to <u>**submit to our agenda, which will affect our security as a chargeback for our fiat paper currency**</u>. Every American will be forced to register or suffer being able to work and earn a living. They will be our chattel, and we will hold the security interest over them forever, by operation of the law merchant under the scheme of secured transactions. Americans, by unknowingly or unwittingly delivering the bills of lading to us will be rendered bankrupt and insolvent, forever to remain economic slaves through taxation, secured by their pledges. <u>**They will be stripped of their rights and given a commercial value designed to make us a profit**</u> and they will be none the wiser, for not one man in a million could ever figure our plans and, if by accident one or two should figure it out, we have in our arsenal <u>**plausible deniability**</u>. After all, this is the only logical way to fund government, **by floating liens and debt to the registrants in the form of <u>benefits and privileges</u>.** This will inevitably reap to us huge profits beyond our wildest expectations and leave every American a contributor to this fraud which we will call "Social Insurance." Without realizing it, every American will insure us for any loss we may incur and in this manner; **every American will unknowingly be our servant**, however begrudgingly. The people will become helpless and without any hope for their redemption and, we will employ the high office of the President of <u>**our dummy corporation**</u> to foment this plot against America."

The United States is bankrupt and its sovereignty is gone. The courts in the U.S. and the States are not solvent thus the Courts and Prosecutors cannot have nor bring a claim against anyone because as a bankrupt entity it has no authority to operate. The U.S. Bankruptcy is expressed in *Franklin-Roosevelt's' Executive Order Numbers: 6073, 6111, and 6260 (See U.S. Senate Report 93-549 pp. 187, 594) under Trading With The Enemy Act of 1917 codified as United-States-Code: Title: 12: Section: 95a: House Joint Resolution 192 of June 5, 1933 C.E. confirmed in Perry-v-U.S. (1933), case site 294 U.S. 330-381 and United-States-Code: Title: 31*

Common Law vs Admiralty vs Statutory Jurisdiction

"If the government was really here to protect your life, liberty, and happiness...then they wouldn't be the first ones trying to take it away"

The Law of the land is called Common Law and the law of the Seas is called Admiralty and Maritime Jurisdiction. One of the major deceptions is that the Government took the law of the seas and superimposed it onto the land (moved the water lines back) without most people not knowing what actually happened. This was done because the European Colonizers were only granted jurisdiction in a ten by ten square mile area (today called

Washington D.C.) but sought to increase their territory and jurisdiction. The Law of the Land (Common Law) was already here in existence and practiced between the highly civilized people who were already here for thousands of years before the Colonists arrived on American soil. The European sailors came from the ocean onto this land so they brought the only jurisdiction that they had (The Law of the Seas/Admiralty and Maritime Jurisdiction) onto the land and governed themselves under that.

In order to disguise what they actually did they decided to call Admiralty Jurisdiction a different name by which today we call **statutory jurisdiction** (Which the Constitution does not mention/allow). The conquest of people here in the Western Hemisphere included getting us to agree either knowingly or unknowingly to their newly created made up statutory jurisdiction (Admiralty and Maritime) and therefore their control.

It is extremely evident when we look at the impact that Admiralty and Maritime Jurisdiction had on the creation of the modern day birth certificates. Remember, that Admiralty and Maritime Jurisdiction are the law of the seas, so in relation, when a ship pulls up to the port it is called being in its "BERTH" spelled with an E. Coincidentally, when a baby comes out of its mother's water it is also called "BIRTH" with an I. The captain also has to let the port authority know what he/she is bringing into this economy (how many cars, tv's, microwaves, etc) by presenting what is called a "CERTIFICATE OF MANIFEST" or a "BERTH CERTIFICATE". Lastly, to help the ship unload it has to be at a "DOCk" and to "unload" a baby you also need a "DOCtor."

Have you wondered why when you walk into the court room you see the stars and stripes flag always with a yellow fringe around the outside? That's because the yellow fringe outline signifies admiralty and maritime jurisdiction. Have you ever wondered why they make you walk through the small waist high double doors swinging when you have to speak to the judge? Because those waist high swinging door symbolize the boarding of a ship and when you board a ship that is exactly how the doors look!

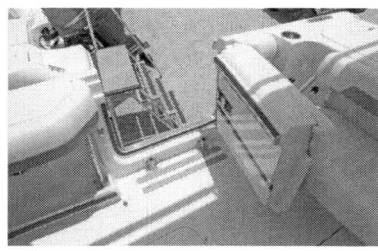

As opposed to Admiralty and Maritime jurisdiction (which has 60,000,000 statues, codes, ordinances, etc) Common Law (the Law of the Land) only has three main principles. Do not harm, steal, or commit fraud against another party. It's common sense and it can be summed up in the golden rule "Do unto others as you would have others do onto you." The problem today is that we were intentionally dumbed down to believe that we have to follow the law of the seas while we are on the land. There are two different jurisdictions that we have today that's Common Law and Admiralty and Maritime Jurisdiction. If you are on the water then you are in Admiralty Jurisdiction and if you are on the land then you are under Common Law jurisdiction. The whole trick was to make you believe that those 60,000,000 statues, codes and ordinances under Admiralty jurisdiction apply to you while you are on the land when in fact they don't! They never old us anything about Common Law jurisdiction because they are and have been making too much money through fines, tickets, and imprisonment by falsely ruling with Admiralty jurisdiction on the land. Even once we learn this information, they use tricks, deceit, and words of art to get us to agree to their jurisdiction without even knowing it. They use things such as the ARTIFICIAL PERSON, walking through the waist high double doors of the court, asking if we *understand* when they really mean "Do you *stand under* my authority?" We have the right to claim Common Law jurisdiction at any time while we are in the court and therefore making the judge look at our case by common law standards (Injury, Loss, or Fraud). We have a right to claim our jurisdiction and if we don't claim Common Law jurisdiction then they assume authority over us and begin adjudicating under Admiralty and Maritime Jurisdiction. If we get a traffic ticket and have not physically harmed, stolen from, or committed fraud on an actual person they we have not committed a crime and the case must be dismissed! There are three elements of a crime and they are the same as the common law principles. The elements of a crime are harm, injury, or loss. Without proving one of these three, there is no crime! They came up with the 60,000,000 statues and got us to unknowingly agree to be governed by them, therefore, causing us to give them our hard working money without even committing actual crimes.

Inasmuch as all law is contract, the contract involved in a constructive trust is an implied contract. An implied contract can be ratified by two (2) means:

> a. Acquiescence by silence, i.e. the *"government"* asserts its intentions concerning your life, rights, and property and you assent, don't rebut, and compliantly go along with what they claim. In 1871 the Government changed the nature of its contract with the people from law as defined by the original Constitution of 1787 that recognizes law

(*common law*), admiralty (*on the sea only*), and equity (*functioning by voluntary contract between all participating parties*), and began relating to people as if they were "*citizens of the Unites States*" within/under the private, commercial, international, military jurisdiction of the new de facto corporation, i.e. *US Inc.* They offered people a "*new deal,*" and almost everyone bought it (*based on naive and foolish trust and assuming that everything was OK*).

The people were thereby denied access to law and placed on the ship of state of *US Inc.* where the captain's word is law and no one has any rights. As Jefferson phrased the matter, "*As government grows, liberty recedes.*"

b. You expressly accept "benefits" offered by the government, and thereby finalize the contract by deed. This is similar to finalizing a contract with a restaurant by sitting down at a table, reading a menu, and then ordering and consuming a meal. By your deeds you affirm to the restaurant that you will pay for the meal in accordance with the price stated on the menu. No written contract is signed, but a contract is formed nevertheless.

By the above two (2) means people give implied assent that they are bound by an alleged contract with *US Inc.* in accordance with the terms and conditions that inhere in being treated as a "*citizen of the United States*" under the 14th Amendment, and are therefore placed into permanent legal status as a *Debtor* and *Surety* for U.S. Inc.. In such a position, people leave the ground of sovereignty and all capacity for asserting their unalienable rights in favor of being presumed as having exercised their sovereignty and free-will autonomy for the purpose of going along with the government's assertion that they sacrifice everything for the *"public good,"* (i.e. *the PCT*). By so doing people lose their standing in law, (i.e. they *"die a civil death in the law."*) They are placed in the legal position of mortmain (i.e. *as if deceased*) and are shorn of capacity for asserting their rights, since the presumption is that they have already exercised those rights for the purpose of being placed in the position they are in, i.e. property of the government with a lien against you and everything your life labor could ever create, including your children. The private being (*the real individual*) is sacrificed for the good of the public (*the imaginary collective*).

When people die such a civil death in the law they are like ghosts, and thereby incapable of managing their own affairs and enjoying their unalienable rights. Like the estate of a decedent, they are then managed by the executors/administrators of the estate, in probate. Such is the condition of every *"citizen of the United States"* today in law, managed by the government agencies acting as executors/administrators of their estates in bankruptcy, legal incapacity, and civil death as assets of the bankrupt US. The US is property of the private *Real Parties of Interest*, the *Creditors in bankruptcy*.

The <u>14th Amendment</u> was allegedly established for the purpose of creating a citizenship for the liberated blacks, and other disenfranchised people, who otherwise had no citizenship because they could not comply with the requirements for state citizenship. What actually happened was that the blacks were taken off of the Southern slave plantations and placed into the slave plantation of *US Inc.*, a far worse lot. The government then gradually absorbed everyone else — including state citizens — into the same condition.

"Moses Parted the Red Sea"

Knowing that Common Law is the Law of the land and Admiralty and Maritime jurisdiction is the law of the seas, think about this:

Moses led his people out from under the oppressive pharaoh (Government) to the Red sea. He and his people were being pursued by the "Authorities" so Moses hit his staff on the ground (claiming common law jurisdiction), therefore, being able to part the sea (admiralty and maritime jurisdiction) and lead his people through safely on the land (common law). Once his people mad it through safely on the land, the sea closed back up and the "Authorities" drowned in their own mess (the deceit of admiralty and maritime jurisdiction on land).

The Bible is full of parables like this one that help us explain and understand what is really going on in today's society.

Natural Person vs. ARTIFICIAL PERSON

With every birth certificate, two things happen. An all CAPITAL LATTERS legal personality or legal fiction (STRAWMAN or ARTIFICIAL PERSON) is created with the same name as you but is not you. Second, the government puts a bond of at least $1,000,000 on each birth certificate and uses it for collateral to back loans and obtain goods but we don't get to access any of the revenue generated by our birth certificate. *But we have found out how, just keep reading!!!!!*

Georgia Code 1-2-1 explains it clearly!!!

O.C.G.A. 1-2-1 (2010)

1-2-1. Classes of persons generally; corporations deemed artificial persons; nature of corporations generally

(a) There are two classes of persons: Natural and ARTIFICIAL.

(b) <u>Corporations are artificial persons</u>. They are creatures of the law and, except insofar as the law forbids it, they are subject to be changed, modified, or destroyed at the will of their creator.

Your straw man (STRAWMAN) is an ARTIFICIAL PERSON created by law at the time of your birth, the inscription of an ALL-CAPITAL LETTERS NAME on your birth certificate/document, which is a document of title and a negotiable instrument. Your lawful name of birthright was replaced with a legal, corporate name of deceit and fraud. Your name in upper and lower-case letters (John Albert Doe *the Natural Person*) has been answering when the legal person, your name in ALL-CAPTIAL LETTERS (JOHN ALBERT DOE), is addressed, and therefore the two have been recognized as being one and the same (when they are not). When, you John Albert Doe, the lawful being distinguish yourself as another party than the ARTIFICIAL LEGAL PERSON, **the two will be separated.**

Once you separate the two, the government's power, the courts power, and the **creditor's powers are all significantly reduced.** I say this because the government only has the power to enforce its will on the STRAWMAN or artificial version of you because the artificial person is classified as a corporation and the United States is ALSO a registered corporation, which are both fictions. Fictions can only deal with other fictions.

The UNITED STATES OF AMERICA is a CORPORATION

Look at the corporate info I found at the Delaware Secretary of State website:

HERE IT IS FOLKS!!!!! THE PROOF!!!!!!

UNITED STATES OF AMERICA, INC.

Non-profit Delaware Corporation Incorporation

File No. 2193946

(LOOK THE FILE NUMBER UP YOURSELF ON GOOGLE!!!!)

CERTIFICATE OF INCORPORATION

of

UNITED STATES OF AMERICA, INC.

FIRST: The name of this corporation is United States of America, Inc.

SECOND: Its registered office in the State of Delaware is to be located at 725 North Market St. City of Wilmington, County of New Castle. The registered agent in charge thereof is The Company Corporation, same address.

THIRD: The nature of the business and the objects and purposes proposed to be transacted, promoted or carried on, are to do any and all the things herein mentioned, as fully and to the same extent as natural persons might or could do, and in any part of the world, viz:

This is a non-stock, non-profit corporation. The purpose of the corporation is to engage in any lawful or activity for which non-profit corporations may be organized under the General Corporation Law of Delaware.

Said corporation is organized exclusively for charitable, religious, education, and scientific purposes, including, for such purposes, the making of distributions to organizations that qualify as exempt organizations under Section 501(c)(3) of the Internal Revenue Code of 1954 (or the corresponding provision of any future United States Internal Revenue Law), to wit:

To promote and foster the development of amateur tournaments and competition; to support athletes in training and development; education and research on amateur sports, both national and international.

FOURTH: The corporation shall not have any capital stock and the conditions of membership shall be stated in the Bylaws.

FIFTH: The name and mailing address of the incorporator is:

Carol Saienni   725 Market Street   Wilmington DE   19801

SIXTH: The powers of the incorporator are to terminate upon filing of the Certificate of Incorporation, the name(s) and mailing address(es) of the persons who are to serve as director(s) until their successors are elected as follows:

Elwood Dees, 5598 College Street, Kings Island, OH 45034-0362

SEVENTH: The activities and affairs of the corporation shall be managed by a Board of Directors. The number of directors which shall constitute the whole Board shall be such as from time to time shall be fixed in the manner provided in the Bylaws, but in no case shall the number be less than one. The directors need not be members of the corporation unless so required by the Bylaws or by Statute. The Board of Directors shall be elected by the members at the annual meeting of the corporation to be held on such date as the Bylaws may provide, and shall hold office until their successors are respectively elected and qualified. The Bylaws shall specify the number of directors necessary to constitute a quorum.

[Image of 1989 Annual Franchise Tax Report, State of Delaware, for "UNITED STATES OF AMERICA, INC.", File Number 2193946, Incorporation Date 04/18/1989, Non-Taxable. Directors: Elwood Dees (5558 College Street Kings I...), Ann Baden (904 N. "E" Street Hamilton,). President: Elwood Dees.]

INTERNAL REVENUE TAX AND AUDIT SERVICE (IRS) For Profit General Delaware Corporation Incorporation date 7/12/**33 File No. 0325720**

FEDERAL RESERVE ASSOCIATION (Federal Reserve) Non-profit Delaware Corporation Incorporation date 9/13/14 **File No. 0042817**

CENTRAL INTELLIGENCE AUTHORITY INC. (CIA) For Profit General Delaware Corporation Incorporation Date 3/9/83 **File No. 2004409**

FEDERAL LAND ACQUISITION CORP. For-profit General Delaware Corporation Incorporation Date 8/22/80 **File No. 0897960**

RTC COMMERCIAL ASSETS TRUST 1995-NP3-2 For-profit Delaware Statutory Trust Incorporation Date 10/24/95 **File No. 2554768**

SOCIAL SECURITY CORP, DEPART. OF HEALTH, EDUCATION AND WELF For-Profit General Delaware Corporation Incorporation date: 11/13/89 **File No. 2213135**

Let's see what the United States Codes say:

28 U.S.C. § 3002: US Code - Section 3002: (15) "United States" means -

(A) A Federal corporation;

(B) An agency, department, commission, board, or other entity Of the United States; or

(C) An instrumentality of the United States.

The 'United States' has always been a "legal fiction" corporation. See: Republica v. Sween, 1 Dallas 43

Let's see what the Bouvier's Law Dictionary has to say: U1: Page 4 of 14

UNITED STATES OF AMERICA
5. The United States of America are a **corporation** endowed with the capacity to sue and be sued, to convey and receive property.
1 Marsh. Dec. 177, 181

"THE UNITED STATES IS A FOREIGN CORPORATION WITH RESPECT TO THE STATE" – Vol 20: Corpus Juris Sect 1785

Fictions can only deal with other fictions, fictions can't interact with things that are real, it's just common sense. **So, they had to create a corporate identity out of your name by putting it in ALL-CAPS on your birth certificate, your driver's license, your traffic tickets, your bills, etc. This was done in order for their corporation (UNITED STATES) to interact with you (Because ALL CAPS signifies a CORPORATION in law)**. Companies have a nine-digit tax id number; your artificial person has a nine-digit social security number (tax id number). Whenever you see BEST BUY, BANK OF AMERICA, SEARS, all of these companies spell their name in ALL-CAPS. All capital letters signifies a corporation in law. Look on your driver's license, your bills, your tickets; they are referring to your artificial person not you! The trick is that they never told you that **legally** there is a **difference** between your name spelled normally in **upper and lower case**, and the way they spell it in **ALL-CAPS**. Starting to make sense? The citizens are considered the "employees" of the Corporation (i.e. Social Security Number/Employee Identification Number).

(THE UNITED STATES IS ***A CORPORATION, NOT A LAND MASS*** AND IT EXISTED BEFORE THE REVOLUTIONARY WAR AND THE BRITISH TROOPS DID NOT LEAVE UNTIL 1796.) *Respublica v. Sweers 1 Dallas 43, Treaty of Commerce 8 Stat 116, The Society for Propagating the Gospel, &c. V. New Haven 8 Wheat 464, Treaty of Peace 8 Stat 80, IRS Publication 6209, Articles of Association October 20, 1774.)*

Legally, since your birth your artificial person (STRAWMAN) has been considered a slave or indentured servant to the various federal, provincial and municipal governments via your STATE-issued, STATE-created birth certificate in the name of your ALL-CAPS person. Your birth certificate was issued so that the issuer could claim "exclusive" title to the legal person created. This was further compounded when you voluntarily obtained a driver's license and a SSN (Social Security Number). The state even owns your personal and private life through your STATE-issued marriage license/certificate issued in the all-caps names. You have had no rights in birth, marriage, nor will you have them even in death (The names on tombstones in cemeteries are in all-caps) unless you understand what it is I'm trying to tell you. The STATE holds the title to your legal person it created via your birth certificate, until John Marshal Doe, the rightful owner, the holder in due course of the instrument, that is yourself, reclaims/redeems it.

Have you ever noticed those red numbers on the bottom left hand side of you birth certificate and wonder what they were there for? It is called a cusip number which is used for security exchange and believe it or not that is the number to your stock on your birth certificate bond! This bond started off a 1,000,000 at birth but now is worth much more because of the revenue generated over the years! We have learned strategies to access that TDA (Treasury Deposit Account) in order to offset any public debts attached to your STRAWMAN, whether it is student loans, car note, mortgage, etc. Also, if you notice on the bottom of your birth certificate it will say "Printed on SECURITY paper." Why would they print your birth certificate on security paper? Because it's a security! A monetizable instrument!

We could ALL sue them for treason but they were smart. They provided us with a remedy, and the law says that if there has been a remedy provided then they can't be sued for treason. The only thing is that they weren't required to tell us what that remedy was, how to find it, or even if we found it, how to use it! Smart plan…. But we found it…HJR 192.

On June 5, 1933, Congress passed House Joint Resolution (HJR 192). HJR 192 was passed to suspend the gold standard and abrogate the gold clause in the national constitution. Since then no one in America has been able to lawfully pay a debt because the only real money is gold. The green pieces of paper we use on a daily basis are not backed by anything like they used to be, they have now become debt notes. You lawfully cannot pay a debt with a debt.

We were never told, openly and clearly with full disclosure of all the facts, that since June 5, 1933, we have been unable to pay our debts. We were never told that we had been pledged (and our children, their children, their children, on and on) as collateral, mere chattel, for the debt created by government officials who committed treason in doing so. We were never told that they quietly and cleverly changed the rules, even the game itself, and that the world we perceive as real is in fact fictional and it's all for their benefit. We were never told that the STRAW MAN (STRAWMAN) a fictional person, a creature of the state is subject to all the codes, statutes, rules, regulations, ordinances, etc. decreed by government, but that WE, the real man and woman (Natural), are not. We were never told we were being treated as property, as slaves, while living in the land of the free and that we could, easily, walk away from the fraud. Knowledge is POWER!!!

When a birth certificate is registered with the U.S. Department of Commerce, it means that the legal person named on it in **FULL CAPS** has become a **surety or guarantor**.

Surety- The person who has pledged him or herself to pay back money or perform a certain action if the principal to a contract fails, as collateral, and as part of the original contract. -- Duhaime's Law Dictionary. 1: a formal engagement (as a pledge) given for the fulfillment of an undertaking. 2: one who promises to answer for the debt or default of another. Under the Uniform Commercial Code, however, a surety includes a guarantor, and the two terms are generally interchangeable. -- Merriam Webster's Dictionary of Law 1996.

Guarantor- A person who pledges collateral for the contract of another, but separately, as part of an independent contract with the obligee of the original contract. -- Duhaime's Law Dictionary.

It's not difficult to see that a state created birth certificate, written with full caps in the name of a legal person, is a document evidencing debt.

This is how it works:

Once each State has registered the birth certificates with the U.S. Department of Commerce the U.S. Department of the Treasury then issues treasury securities in the form of treasury bonds, notes, and bills (**using the birth certificates as sureties or guarantors** for these bonds, notes and bills/dollar bills). The value of the birth certificate is based on the future tax revenues of your legal person (STRAWMAN). This means that the bankrupt corporate U.S. can guarantee to the purchasers of their securities the lifetime labor and tax revenues of all Americans as collateral for payment! They simply do this by converting the **lawful name** (Adam Speaks) into a **legal person** (ADAM SPEAKS).

Legally, you are considered a slave or indentured servant to the various federal, state and local governments via your STATE issued and created birth certificate in the name of your full caps person. The reason this birth certificate was issued is so that they hold the title of birth to your legal person.

This is compounded further when one voluntarily obtains a driver's license or a Social Security Identification number. They own even your personal and private life through your STATE issued marriage certificate issued in the names of "legal persons". You have no rights in birth, marriage, or even death. They hold the sovereign right to all legal fiction titles they have created under this "legal" scheme.

"Marriage is a civil contract to which there are three parties-the husband, the wife and the **state**." Van Koten v. Van Koten. 154 N.E. 146.

Our current problem is that we have **voluntarily** agreed to their system of legal fiction by CONTRACT (driver's license, social security card, registration, birth certificate and simply just remaining silent, a legal default) and not taking claim to our own inalienable rights.

"Right To Travel vs. Driver's License"

(They NEVER told you that there is a HUGE difference between **Driving** and **Traveling**!!!)

All government officials, including local policemen and firemen in every city and borough, **MUST** take an Official Oath on the Constitution. If the Natural people and Citizens lack knowledge, they will often <u>fail to recognize</u> when an "Ordinance" or "Statute", passed by politicians, violates the "**Supreme Law of the Land**". No Ordinances or Statutes, or Laws of any of the several States, can contradict or violate the Supreme Law of The Land (See Article VI U.S. Constitution) and be held as Constitutional.

<u>"DESPITE ACTIONS OF POLICE AND LOCAL COURTS,</u>

<u>HIGHER COURTS HAVE RULED THAT AMERICAN CITIZENS</u>

<u>HAVE A RIGHT TO TRAVEL WITHOUT STATE PERMITS"</u>

Here are some Definitions to consider:

Black's Law Dictionary: **Driver** – One **EMPLOYED** in conducting or operating a coach, carriage, wagon, or other vehicle, with horses, mules, or other animals, or a bicycle, tricycle, or motor car, though not a street railroad car. See Davis v. Petrinovich, 112 Ala. 654, 21 So. 344, 36 L.R.A. 615; Isaacs v. Railroad Co., 7 Am. Rep. 418, 47 N.Y. 122.

Black's Law Dictionary, 3rd Ed

"The activity licensed by state DMVs and in connection with which individuals must submit personal information to the DMV – the operation of <u>MOTOR VEHICLES</u> – is itself integrally related to interstate **COMMERCE**".

Seth Waxman, Solicitor General
U.S. Department of Justice

Motor vehicle means every description of carriage or other contrivance propelled or drawn by mechanical power and used for **COMMERCIAL PURPOSES** on the highways in the transportation of passengers, passengers and property, or property or cargo;

Motor vehicle – Laws of Florida c. 14764 (1931) The term "motor vehicle" shall include all vehicles or machines propelled by any power other than muscular used upon the public highways (but not over fixed rails) for the transportation of persons or property **FOR COMPENSATION** either as common carriers, private contract carriers or for hire carriers.

If you see, the above things I underlined in those definitions were, **"EMPLOYEED"**, **"COMMERCE"**, **"COMMERCIAL PURPOSES"** and **"FOR COMPENSATION"** because *driving* a *motor vehicle* in LAW means getting **PAID** (commerce/commercial purposes) while using the public roads. Like a <u>truck driver</u>, <u>cab driver</u>, <u>limo driver</u>, etc. These people **do**

need licenses to "Drive" on the roads. On the other hand, **if you are just going to the grocery store, or your friend's house, then you are lawfully *traveling* and not driving. That's the difference!**

For years professionals within the criminal justice system have acted on the belief that traveling by motor vehicle **was a privilege** that was given to a citizen only after approval by their state government in the form of a permit or license to drive. In other words, the individual must be granted the privilege before his use of the state highways was considered legal. Legislators, police officers, and court officials are becoming aware that there are court decisions that disprove the belief that driving is a privilege and therefore DOES NOT require government approval in the form of a license. Presented here are some of these cases:

CASE #1: "The use of the highway for the purpose of travel and transportation is not a mere privilege, but a common fundamental right of which the public and individuals cannot rightfully be deprived." *Chicago Motor Coach v. Chicago, 169 NE 221.*

CASE #2: "The right of the citizen to travel upon the public highways and to transport his property thereon, either by carriage or by automobile, is not a mere privilege which a city may prohibit or permit at will, but a common law right which he has under the right to life, liberty, and the pursuit of happiness." *Thompson v. Smith, 154 SE 579.*

It could not be stated more directly or conclusively that citizens of the states have a common law right to travel, without approval or restriction (license), and that this right is protected under the U.S Constitution.

CASE #3: "The right to travel is a part of the liberty of which the citizen cannot be deprived without due process of law under the Fifth Amendment." *Kent v. Dulles, 357 US 116, 125.*

CASE #4: "**The right to travel is a well-established common right that does not owe its existence to the federal government. It is recognized by the courts as a natural right.**" *Schactman v. Dulles 96 App DC 287, 225 F2d 938, at 941.*

Think of it like this. A cowboy rides through town and is confronted by the sheriff. He says to the sheriff "just **traveling**/passing through sheriff", or he has his cows and is [**driving**] his cows across the land." **When driving you are involved in the act of commerce and traveling simultaneously**.

Samuel E Roher, a Berks County Republican candidate for U.S. Senate argued in 2006 that the state has no legal authority to require people to get driver's licenses and register their cars.

He also wrote that driver licensing and vehicle registration should be abolished, saying the state Vehicle Code only applies to **commercial traffic**. He also compared the requirements to slavery because both restrict an individual's freedom to travel.

Rohrer wrote in support of constituent William Reil, a longtime acquaintance who was found guilty in 2006 of vehicle offenses including driving with a suspended license saying:

"Mr. Reil's use of an automobile is simply an extension of his personal liberty to move about as he wishes," Rohrer wrote. "An individual who wishes to utilize an automobile or other means of conveyance in order to exercise his right to travel cannot lawfully be required to obtain a license to drive or to register his automobile in order to operate it freely on our roads."

In defending Mr. Reil, Mr. Rohrer said he had a lawyer on his legislative staff "examine Mr. Reil's understanding of this complex issue." The staff member found Mr. Reil's arguments were based on "solid legal precedent," Mr. Rohrer wrote.

"I have also performed my own in-depth research over the years and I, too, have reached the conclusion that Mr. Reil stands on solid legal footing," Mr. Rohrer wrote.

The "crux of the issue," he wrote, is whether the state Vehicle Code applies to an individual. His staff's research showed it only applies to **"commercial vehicles and commercial use of the roads."**

"If one's movement can be restrained, such restraint is intrinsically a restraint of his liberty. Mr. Reil's use of an automobile is simply an extension of his personal liberty to move about as he wishes," Mr. Rohrer wrote**. "An individual who wishes to utilize an automobile or other means of conveyance in order to exercise his right to travel cannot lawfully be required to obtain a license to drive or to register his automobile in order to operate it freely on our roads."**

Mr. Rohrer wrote that he knew his conclusion would have "vast implications." He also stated, "I am well aware that a ruling of this nature would **'undo'** years of enforcement of our existing laws. I am also well aware of **the enormous economic impact** such a ruling would have on the Department of Transportation," he wrote. In the interview, Mr. Rohrer said he got involved in the case at Mr. Reil's request. He remembered joining several other legislators at a meeting with state Department of Transportation officials where the rationale for licensing and registering vehicles was discussed.

When asked if he still believes what he wrote in the letter about licensing and registration, Mr. Rohrer did not back off.

"I think what you have … is that if you look at law, the law governing commercial activity, commercial traffic … that is very, very clear in law – that licensing, permitting, taxing, a number of those things are established under commercial law because commercial activities and corporations are a creature of the state," he said.

As long as the state does not go too far in restricting their activity, it has "the freedom" to restrict, he said. "Individuals, though, there was no precedent in law … and in essence, **what we were told as House members is that the**

application of the commercial law was essentially flipped down on top of an individual."

"The right to travel is an inherent constitutional right," he said.

As a legislator, Mr. Rohrer said, he had an obligation to a constituent to examine the issue and ask the judge to weigh the argument when making her decision. Randy DeSoto, a spokesman for Republican Senate candidate Marc Scaringi, said he partly agreed with Mr. Rohrer. Mr. Scaringi believes "the right to travel and to earn a living is a God-given, fundamental right that the state should not be able to deny," Mr. DeSoto said in a prepared statement.

One of the main violations on our inalienable RIGHT TO TRAVEL is the driver's license and the "routine" traffic stop/ traffic ticket. A driver's license **ONLY** verifies that you have a **CONTRACT** with a **PRIVATE** corporation (DMV) that politicians have a contract with. They get a kickback for helping to rob you by forcing you into contracts with the PRIVATE institution (DMV), which they don't have the power or authority to do...but they did it!

As hard as it is for those in law enforcement to believe, there is no room for speculation in these court decisions. **American citizens do indeed have the inalienable right to use the roadways unrestricted in any manner as long as they are not damaging or violating property** or rights of others. Government, in requiring the people to obtain drivers licenses, and accepting vehicle inspections and DUI/DWI roadblocks without question, is restricting, and therefore violating the people's common law right to travel.

Is this a new legal interpretation on this subject? Apparently not. This means **that the beliefs and opinions our state legislators, the courts, and those in law enforcement have acted upon for years have been in error.** Researchers armed with **actual facts** state that case law is overwhelming in determining that to restrict the movement of the individual in the free exercise of his right to travel is a serious breach of those freedoms secured by the U.S. Constitution and most state constitutions. That means it is unlawful. *The revelation that the American citizen has always had the inalienable right to travel raises profound questions for those who are involved in making and enforcing state laws.* The first of such questions may very well be this: If the states have been enforcing laws that are unconstitutional on their face, it would seem that there must be some way that a state can legally put restrictions (such as licensing requirements, mandatory insurance, vehicle registration, vehicle inspections, etc) on a citizen's constitutionally protected rights.

For the answer, let us look, once again, to the U.S. courts for a determination of this very issue. In *Hertado v. California, 110 US 516,* the U.S Supreme Court states very plainly:

"The state cannot diminish rights of the people."

And in *Bennett v. Boggs, 1 Baldw 60,*

"Statutes that violate the plain and obvious principles of common right and common reason are null and void."

These judicial decisions are straight to the point, there is no lawful method for government to put restrictions or limitations on rights belonging to the people. Other cases are even more straight forward:

"The assertion of federal rights, when plainly and reasonably made, is not to be defeated under the name of local practice." *Davis v. Wechsler, 263 US 22, at 24*

"Where rights secured by the Constitution are involved, there can be no rule making or legislation which would abrogate them." *Miranda v. Arizona, 384 US 436, 491.*

"The claim and exercise of a constitutional right cannot be converted into a crime." *Miller v. US, 230 F 486, at 489.*

"There can be no sanction or penalty imposed upon one because of this exercise of constitutional rights." *Sherer v. Cullen, 481 F 946*

I could go on quoting court decision after court decision; however, the Constitution itself already answers our question. Can a government legally put restrictions on the rights of the American people at any time, for any reason? The answer is found in Article Six of the U.S. Constitution:

"This Constitution, and the Laws of the United States which shall be made in Pursuance thereof; **shall be the supreme Law of the Land; and the Judges in every State shall be bound thereby, any Thing in the Constitution or laws of any State to the Contrary not one word withstanding.**"

In the same Article, it says just who within our government that is bound by this Supreme Law:

"The Senators and Representatives before mentioned, and the Members of the several State Legislatures, and all executive and judicial Officers, both of the United States and of the several States, shall be bound by Oath or Affirmation, to support this Constitution..."

Here's an interesting question. **Is ignorance of these laws an excuse for such acts by officials?** If we are to follow the letter of the law, (as we are sworn to do), this places officials who involve themselves in such unlawful acts in an unfavorable legal situation. For it is a felony and federal crime to violate or deprive citizens of their constitutionally protected rights. Our system of law dictates that there are only two ways to legally remove a right belonging to the people. These are:

1. **By Lawfully amending the Constitution, or**

2. **By a person KNOWINGLY waiving a particular right...(PERIOD!!)**

Some of the confusion on our present system has arisen because *many millions* of people have waived their **right to travel** unrestricted and **volunteered** into the jurisdiction of the state **unknowingly**. Those who have given up these rights are now legally regulated by state law and *must* acquire the proper permits and registrations. There are basically two groups of people in this category:

1. Citizens who involve themselves in commerce upon the highways of the state. Here is what the courts have said about this: "...For while a citizen has the right to travel upon the public highways and to transport his property thereon, that right does not extend to the use of the highways...**as a place for private gain**. For the latter purpose, no person has a vested right to use the highways of this state, but it is a privilege...which the (state) may grant or withhold at its discretion..." *State v. Johnson, 245 P 1073.*

    There are many court cases that confirm and point out the difference between the right of the citizen to travel, and a government privilege, and there are numerous other court decisions that spell out the jurisdiction issue in these two ***distinctly different*** activities.

2. The second group of citizens that is legally under the jurisdiction of the state are those citizens who have knowingly or unknowingly waived their right to travel

unregulated and unrestricted by requesting placement under such jurisdiction through the acquisition of a state driver's license, vehicle registration, mandatory insurance, etc. (In other words, by contract.) We should remember what makes this legal and not a violation of the common law right to travel is that they knowingly **volunteer by contract** to waive their rights. If they were forced, coerced or unknowingly placed under the state's powers, the courts have said it is a clear violation of their rights. This in itself raises a very interesting question. ***What percentage of the people in each state have applied for and received licenses, registrations and obtained insurance after erroneously being advised by their government that it was mandatory?***

Many of our courts, attorneys and police officials are just becoming informed about this important issue and the difference between privileges and rights. We can assume that the majority of those Americans carrying state licenses and vehicle registrations have no knowledge of the rights they waived in obeying laws such as these that the U.S. Constitution clearly states are unlawful, i.e. laws of no effect - laws that are not laws at all but operate under the "Color of Law".

An area of serious consideration for every police officer is to understand that the most important law in our land which he or she has taken an oath to protect, defend, and enforce, **is not** state laws and city or county ordinances, but the law that supersedes all other laws **the U.S. Constitution**. If laws in a particular state or local community conflict with the supreme law of our nation, **there is no question that the officer's duty is to uphold the U.S. Constitution.**

Every police officer should keep the following U.S. court ruling in mind before issuing citations concerning licensing, registration, and insurance:

"The claim and exercise of a constitutional right cannot be converted into a crime." *Miller v. US, 230 F 486, 489.*

And as we have seen, traveling freely, going about one's daily activities, is the exercise of a most basic right.

and ...

"There can be no sanction or penalty imposed upon one because of this exercise of constitutional Rights."

Snerer vs. Cullen, 481 F. 946

Corpus Delicti= "NO INJURY, NO DAMAGE, NO CRIME!!!"

(There is no Injured Party when you are issued a traffic ticket!)

Let me begin this section with an experience that I had with a student of mine. This particular student learned the concepts and key facts that were needed to protect herself from these traffic courts (rackets). She had received three citations and was asked to appear in court. Knowing that her court is her paperwork she took my direction and filled a Demurer (Motion to Dismiss) letting the court know that they did not have standing to bring forth these tickets to her at all. She stated that the courts did not have a valid cause of action to charge her. She was able to do this because the courts classify traffic tickets (no matter how minor) as criminal. HERE'S THE CATCH!!!! Over 90% of us don't actually know what a crime actually consists of (the actual legal definition). A crime has to inflict HARM, INJURY, or LOSS. Now her traffic tickets were from the STATE OF FLORIDA and classified under criminal. Now that raises another question. How can you harm or injure the STATE OF FLORIDA? You can't! They have to produce what is called a ***Corpus delicti*** or actual injured party...and they can't!!!

Without a valid cause of action there's no corpus delicti. If there's no corpus delicti a case has no standing.

Supreme courts ruled "Without Corpus delicti there can be no crime." "In every prosecution for crime it is necessary to establish the "corpus delicti", i.e., the body or elements of the crime." People v. Lopez, 62 Ca. Rptr. 47, 254 C.A.2d 185.

Corpus delicti (plural: corpora delicti) (Latin: "**body of crime**") is a term from Western jurisprudence referring to the principle that a crime must have been proven to have occurred before a person can be convicted of committing that crime. Black's Law Dictionary (6th ed.) defines "*corpus delicti*" as: "the fact of a crime having been actually committed."

1.   The corpus delicti is related to standing and must be proven in every prosecution and has two elements:

a. "The corpus delicti of a crime consists of two elements: (1) the fact of **_the injury or loss or harm_**, and (2) the existence of a criminal agency as its cause [citations omitted] there must be sufficient proof of both elements of the corpus delicti beyond a reasonable doubt." 29A American Jurisprudence Second Ed., Evidence § 1476.

b. "**Proof of the *corpus delicti* is required in all criminal cases**...There are three basic elements in the proof of a crime: (1) the occurrence of **loss or injury**, (2) criminal causation of that loss or injury and (3) the identity of the defendant as the perpetrator of the crime. However, it is firmly established in this State that the term corpus delicti embraces only the first two of these elements-loss or injury and criminal causation." State v. Hill, 221 A.2d 725, 728 (NJ)

One of the major points that you should understand is **corpus delicti**. It is very important because we pay numerous tickets and spend time in jail be because we don't understand this element of due process.

Below are the three cases that my student had <u>DISMISSED</u>!

They were dismissed because of what she learned about the courts not having a valid cause of action because of no corpus delicti. I wrote a Demurrer (Motion to Dismiss) on her behalf and we filed it before her court date allowing the court enough time to review her points in her Affidavit. After reviewing her paperwork, she showed up to court and right away her cases were all dismissed! VICTORY!!!!

Hillsborough County Traffic Court   2/15/2013

MUNI CODE: 4   VB: 14 CT:
*PLEA: G _____   NG __
WAIVED SPEEDY TRIAL _____
CONTINUED TO _____
FOR: A____ H____ T____

CITATION: 006593WKL   CASE NO: C1214222098

*VERDICT: *SENTENCE:
G   JAIL
NG   SUSP
(BSH)   JAIL/SUSP
EST   PROB
NOL PRO   OTHER
JUV   *SCHOOL:
W/H   DDS   DUI
OTHER   *LIC ACTIC
                  LIC REV

NAME: RAMOS, LOURDES DE MARIA
320.261   ATTACHING TAG NOT ASSIGND   C

OFFENSE DATE: 11/16/2012   BIRTH DATE 02/03/1977
SPEEDY TRL DT: 02/14/2013   DL: R520524775430
SEX: Female   RACE: White   HGT: 5 ft 2
STV=CHARGE NO   ACCIDENT TYPE: PD
DAMAGE: $20,000.00   BREATH TEST: %
SPEED POSTED: ACTUAL: DR / OWN

SET FOR NONJURYTRIAL ON: 02/28/2013
IN COURT ROOM NO: 23   AT   8:00 A.M.
DIV: D   JUDGE: DICK GRECO, JR
LEO: JEREMY HOUSE   AGENCY: HCSO
CAPIAS: NO   CONTINUANCES: 1   DELINQ: 1
D6:   NONE

FINE _____
ADDL CC _____
MANDATORY: $215.00
PROSEC: $50.00
PD LIEN: _____
PD APP FEE: _____
TOTAL _____
TAKE FROM BOND? YES
ISSUE D6 _____ CA
NOTES: _____

BOND TYPE: S   AMT: $250.00   STATUS: ACTIVE
BOND PERSON: ARMANDO ARCOS BAIL BONDS
WITNESSES   NO: 0

WITH/WITHOUT INTERPRETER
ATTORNEY:
PRESENT: YES/NO

BY JUDGE _____

Hillsborough County Traffic Court   2/15/2013

MUNI CODE: 4   VB: 1
*PLEA: G
WAIVED SPEEDY TRIAL
CONTINUED TO _____
FOR: A____ H____ T

CITATION: 006593WKK   CASE NO: I214223330
NAME: RAMOS, LOURDES DE MARIA
316.066(1)D   FAILURE OF EACH PARTY TO PROVIDE
             PROOF OF INSURANCE

*VERDICT:	*SENTE
G	JAIL
NG	SUSP
DISM	JAIL/SL
	PROB
EST	OTHER
NOL PRO	*SCHO
JUV	DDS
W/H	*LIC A
OTHER	LIC RE

OFFENSE DATE: 11/16/2012   BIRTH DATE 02/03/1977
SPEEDY TRL DT: 05/15/2013   DL: R520524775430
SEX: Female   RACE: White   HGT: 5 ft 2
STV=CHARGE   NO   ACCIDENT TYPE: PD
DAMAGE: $20,000.00   BREATH TEST: %
SPEED POSTED: ACTUAL: DR / DWN

FINE $30.00
ADDL CC _____
MANDATORY: $73.0

SET FOR DISPO ON: 02/28/2013
IN COURT ROOM NO: 23   AT   8:00 A.M.
DIV: D   JUDGE: DICK GRECO, JR
LEO: JEREMY HOUSE   AGENCY: HCSO
CAPIAS: NO   CONTINUANCES: 1   DELINQ: 0
D6:   NONE

PD LIEN: _____
TOTAL
TAKE FROM BOND? YE
ISSUE D6
NOTES:

BOND TYPE: AMT: _____   STATUS: []
BOND PERSON:

WITNESSES   NO: 0

WITH/WITHOUT INTERPRETER
ATTORNEY:
PRESENT: YES/NO

BY JUDGE _____

As you can see, if the courts cannot provide proof of the "corpus delicti" (actual harm, injury, or loss) then there is NO CRIME. Knowing this, we have to ask ourselves, "Why are we fined and imprisoned for minor traffic violations?" We are treated this way because of a lack of knowledge! The courts cannot produce a corpus delicti because the plaintiff in most traffic cases is "THE STATE OF _____" vs (YOUR NAME).

You can not harm or injure THE STATE OF _____ because it is a fictitious corporation (ARTIFICIAL PERSON), therefore, without corpus delicti there cannot be a crime committed. Below are some Supreme Court decisions and other case law for you to review:

"In every criminal trial, the prosecution must prove the corpus delicti, or the body of the crime itself-i.e., the fact of **injury, loss or harm**, and the existence of a criminal agency as its cause." People v. Sapp, 73 P.3d 433, 467 (Cal. 2003) [quoting People v. Alvarez, (2002) 27 Cal.4th 1161, 1168-1169, 119 Cal.Rptr.2d 903, 46 P.3d 372.].

"Elements of "corpus delicti," injury or loss or harm and a criminal agency which causes such injury, loss or harm, need only be proven by a "reasonable probability," i.e., by slight or prima facie proof..." People v. Ramirez, 153 Cal.Rptr. 789, 791, 91 C.A. 132.

""Corpus delicti" of crime consists of fact of injury, loss, or harm, and existence of criminal agency as cause." People v. Daly, 10 Cal.Rptr.2d 21, 28, 8 CA4th 47.

"Generally, "corpus delicti" of crime is (1) the fact of the loss or harm, and (2) the existence of a criminal agency as its cause." People v. Dorsey, 118 Cal.Rptr. 362, 43 CA3d 953.

"The corpus delicti of a crime consists of two elements [:] the fact of the injury or loss or harm, and the existence of a criminal agency as its cause." People v. Jones, 949 P.2d 890, 902, 70 Cal.Rptr.2d 793, 17 Cal.4th 279.

"The corpus delicti rule requires that the corpus delicti or the body or substance of the crime charged be proved independent from the accused's extrajudicial confession or admissions. The corpus delicti of a crime consists of two elements: (1) the fact of the injury or loss or harm, and (2) the existence of a criminal agency as its cause. [citing] People v Jennings, 53 Cal 3d 334

"As a general principal, standing to invoke the judicial process requires an actual justiciable controversy as to which the complainant has a real interest in the ultimate adjudication because he or she has either suffered or is about to suffer an injury." People v. Superior Court, 126 Cal.Rptr.2d 793.

So, as you can see, there are numerous cases/ supreme court cases that have said the same thing that I am saying, **"If there is no injury, there is no crime!" Make sure you demand the "Corpus Delicti" because in a traffic court they CAN NOT produce it!!!** You can never injure the STATE OF _____ because it is not flesh and blood, it is a corporation! KNOWLEDGE IS POWER!!!!!!!

POLICE POWER

It is not the duty of the police to <u>protect you</u>. Their job is to protect the Corporation and arrest code breakers. Sappv. Tallahassee, 348 So. 2nd 363, Reiff v. City of Philadelphia, 477 F. Supp. 1262, Lynch v. N.C. Dept. of Justice 376 S.E. 2nd. 247.

The confusion of the police power with the power of taxation (tickets), usually arises in cases where the police power has affixed a penalty to a certain act, or where it requires licenses to be obtained and a certain sum be paid for certain occupations. The power used in the instant case cannot, however, be the power of taxation since an attempt to levy a tax upon a Right would be open to Constitutional objection.

Each law relating to the use of police power must ask three questions:

>"1. Is there threatened danger?

>"2. Does a regulation involve a Constitutional Right?

>"3. Is this regulation reasonable?

People vs. Smith, 108 Am.St.Rep. 715;

Bovier's Law Dictionary, 1914 ed., under "*Police Power*"

When applying these three questions to the statute in question, some very important issues emerge. First, "*is there a threatened danger*" in the individual using his automobile on the public highways, in the ordinary course of life and business?

The answer is No! There is nothing inherently dangerous in the use of an automobile when it is carefully managed. Their guidance, speed, and noise are subject to a quick and easy control, under a competent and considerate manager, it is as harmless on the road as a horse and buggy.

It is the manner of managing the automobile, and that alone, which threatens the safety of the public. The ability to stop quickly and to respond quickly to guidance would seem to make the automobile one of the least dangerous conveyances. (See **Yale Law Journal**, December, 1905.)

"The automobile is not inherently dangerous."

Cohens vs. Meadow, 89 SE 876;
Blair vs. Broadmore, 93 SE 532

To deprive all persons of the Right to use the road in the ordinary course of life and business, because one might, in the future, become dangerous, would be a deprivation not only of the Right to travel, but also the Right to due process. (See "*Due Process*,")

Next, does the regulation involve a Constitutional Right? This question has already been addressed and answered previously, and need not be reinforced other than to remind you that the Citizen does have the Right to travel upon the public highway by automobile in the ordinary course of life and business. It can therefore be concluded that this regulation does involve a Constitutional Right.

The third question is the most important in this case. "*Is this regulation reasonable?*" **The answer is No!** The licensing statute is oppressive and could be effectively administered by less oppressive means.

Although the **Fourteenth Amendment** does not interfere with the proper exercise of the police power, in accordance with the general principle that **the power must be exercised so as not to invade unreasonably the rights guaranteed by the United States Constitution**, it is established beyond question that every state power, including the police power, is limited by the **Fourteenth Amendment** (and others) and by the inhibitions there imposed.

Therefore, the ultimate test of the propriety of police power regulations must be found in the **Fourteenth Amendment**, since it operates to limit the field of the police power to the extent of preventing the enforcement of statutes in denial of Rights that the Amendment protects. (See **Parks vs. State**, 64 NE 682.)

"With regard, particularly to the U.S. Constitution, it is elementary that a Right secured or protected

by that document cannot be overthrown or impaired by any state police authority."

Connolly vs. Union Sewer Pipe Co., 184 US 540;

Lafarier vs. Grand Trunk R.R. Co., 24 A. 848;

O'Neil vs. Providence Amusement Co., 108 A. 887

"The police power of the state must be exercised in subordination to the provisions of the U.S. Constitution."

Bacahanan vs. Wanley, 245 US 60;

Panhandle Eastern Pipeline Co. vs. State Highway Commission, 294 US 613

> *"It is well settled that the Constitutional Rights protected from invasion by the police power, include Rights safeguarded both by express and implied prohibitions in the Constitutions."*

Tiche vs. Osborne, 131 A. 60

> *"As a rule, fundamental limitations of regulations under the police power are found in the spirit of the Constitutions, not in the letter, although they are just as efficient as if expressed in the clearest language."*

Mehlos vs. Milwaukee, 146 NW 882

As it applies in the instant case, the language of the **Fifth Amendment** is clear:

"No person shall be ... deprived of Life, Liberty, or Property without due process of law."

As has been shown, the courts at all levels have firmly established an absolute Right to travel. In the instant case, the state, by applying commercial statutes to all entities, natural and artificial persons alike, has deprived this free and natural person of the **Right of Liberty**, without cause and without due process of law.

DUE PROCESS

*"The essential elements of due process of law are ... **Notice** and The Opportunity to defend."*

Simon vs. Craft, 182 US 427

Even though we have this case law "Simon vs. Craft", **not one individual has been given notice of the loss of his/her Right, let alone before signing the license (contract). Nor was the Citizen given any opportunity to defend against the loss of his/her right to travel, by automobile, on the**

highways, in the ordinary course of life and business. This amounts to an arbitrary deprivation of Liberty.

> "There should be no arbitrary deprivation of Life or Liberty ..."

Barbour vs. Connolly, 113 US 27, 31;

Yick Wo vs. Hopkins, 118 US 356

and ...

> "The right to travel is part of the Liberty of which a citizen cannot deprived without due process of law under the Fifth Amendment. This Right was emerging as early as the Magna Carta."

Kent vs. Dulles, 357 US 116 (1958)

The focal point of this question of police power and due process must balance upon the point of making the public highways a safe place for the public to travel. If a man travels in a manner that creates actual damage, an action would lie (*civilly*) for recovery of damages. The state could then also proceed against the individual to deprive him of his Right to use the public highways, for cause. This process would fulfill the due process requirements of the **Fifth Amendment** while at the same time insuring that Rights guaranteed by the U.S. Constitution and the state constitutions would be protected.

But unless or until harm or damage (*a crime*) is committed, there is no cause for interference in the private affairs or actions of a Citizen.

> "*Where rights secured by the Constitution are involved, there can be no rule making or legislation which would abrogate them.*"

Miranda vs. Arizona, 384 US 436, 491

Thus, the legislature does not have the power to abrogate the Citizen's Right to travel upon the public roads, by passing legislation forcing the citizen to waive his Right and convert that Right into a privilege. Furthermore, we have previously established that this *"privilege"* has been defined as applying only to those who are *"conducting business in the streets"* or *"operating for-hire vehicles."*

The legislature has attempted (*by legislative fiat*) to deprive the Citizen of his Right to use the roads in the ordinary course of life and business, without affording the Citizen the safeguard of *"due process of law."*

SURRENDER OF RIGHTS

A Citizen cannot be forced to give up his/her Rights in the name of regulation.

> "... the only limitations found restricting the right of the state to condition the use of the public highways as a means of vehicular transportation for compensation are **(1)** that the state must not exact of those it permits to use the highways for hauling for gain that they surrender any of their inherent U.S. Constitutional Rights as a condition precedent to obtaining permission for such use ..."

Riley vs. Laeson, 142 So. 619;

Stephenson vs. Binford, supra.

CONVERSION OF A RIGHT TO A CRIME

As previously demonstrated, the Citizen has the Right to travel and to transport his property upon the public highways in the ordinary course of life and business. However, if one exercises this Right to travel (without first giving up the Right and converting that Right into a privilege) the Citizen is by "statute", guilty of a crime. This amounts to converting the exercise of a Constitutional Right into a crime.

Recall the **Miller vs. U.S.** and **Snerer vs. Cullen**

"The state cannot diminish Rights of the people."

Hurtado vs. California, 110 US 516

and ...

> "Where rights secured by the Constitution are involved, there can be no rule making or legislation which would abrogate them."

<u>Miranda</u>, supra.

So, we can see that any attempt by the legislature to make the act of using the public highways as a matter of Right into a crime, is void upon its face. Any person who claims his Right to travel upon the highways, and so exercises that Right, cannot be tried for a crime of doing so.

As we have already shown, the term "*drive*" can only apply to those who are **<u>employed in the business of transportation for hire</u>**. It has been shown that FREEDOM includes the Citizen's Right to use the public highways in the ordinary course of life and business without license or regulation by the police powers of the state.

The courts are "*duty bound*" to recognize and stop the "*stealthy encroachments*" which have been made upon the Citizen's Right to travel and to use the roads to transport his property in the "*ordinary course of life and business*." The court also must recognize that the Right to travel is part of the Liberty of which a Citizen cannot be deprived without specific cause and without the "*due process of law*" guaranteed in the **<u>Fifth Amendment</u>**.

The history of this "*invasion*" of the Citizen's Right to use the public highways shows clearly that the legislature simply found a source of untapped revenue, got greedy, and attempted to enforce a statute in an unconstitutional manner upon those free and natural individuals who have a Right to travel upon the highways. This was not attempted in an outright action, but in a slow, meticulous, calculated encroachment upon the Citizen's Right to travel.

This position must be accepted unless the prosecutor can show his authority for the position that the "*use of the road in the ordinary course of life and business*" is somehow a privilege.

To rule in any other manner, without clear authority for an adverse ruling, will infringe upon fundamental and basic concepts of Constitutional law. This position, that a Right cannot be regulated under any guise, must be accepted without concern for the monetary loss of the state.

> "*Disobedience or evasion of a Constitutional Mandate cannot be tolerated, even though such disobedience may, at least temporarily, promote in some respects the best interests of the public.*"

Slote vs. Examination, 112 ALR 660

and ...

> "*Economic necessity cannot justify a disregard of Constitutional guarantee.*"

Riley vs. Carter, 79 ALR 1018;

16 Am. Jur. (2nd), Const. Law, Sect. 81

and ...

> "*Constitutional Rights cannot be denied simply because of hostility to their assertions and exercise; vindication of conceded Constitutional Rights cannot be made dependent upon any theory that it is less expensive to deny them than to afford them.*"

Watson vs. Memphis, 375 US 526

Therefore, the Court's decision in the instant case must be made without the issue of cost to the state being taken into consideration, as that issue is irrelevant. The state cannot lose money that it never had a right to demand from the "*Sovereign People*."

Now we come to the issue of "*public policy*." It could be argued that the "*licensing scheme*" of all persons is a matter of "*public policy*." However, if this argument is used, it too must fail, as:

> "No public policy of a state can be allowed to override the positive guarantees of the U.S. Constitution."

16 Am.Jur. (2nd), Const. Law, Sect. 70

So even "*public policy*" cannot abrogate this Citizen's Right to travel and to use the public highways in the ordinary course of life and business.

Therefore, it must be concluded that:

> "We have repeatedly held that the legislature may regulate the use of the highways for carrying on business for private gain and that such regulation is a valid exercise of the police power."

Northern Pacific R.R. Co., supra.

and ...

> "The act in question is a valid regulation, and as such is binding upon all who use the highway for the purpose of private gain."

Any other construction of this statute would render it unconstitutional as applied to this Citizen or any Citizen. There is no notice is given to people applying for driver's (*or other*) licenses that they have a perfect right to use the roads without any permission, and that they surrender valuable rights by taking on the regulation system of licensure.

Few (if any) people who apply for a driver's license intentionally surrender their inalienable rights. They are told that they **must** have the license. As we have seen, **this is not the case.**

No one in their right mind voluntarily surrenders complete liberty and accepts in its place a set of regulations.

"The people never give up their liberties but under some delusion."

<u>Edmund Burke</u>, (1784)

Article 13 of the Universal Declaration of Human Rights states:

- (1) **Everyone has the right to freedom of movement** and residence within the borders of each state.
- (2) Everyone has the right to leave any country, including his own, and to return to his country.

Arizona Senator's Letter to State Officials

On December 10, 1985, Arizona State Senator Wayne Stump addressed a letter to the State's Director of Public Safety, Ralph Milstead, explaining how members of his state were rescinding their contracts with the state (drivers license). The same letter was addressed to the sheriff of every county, every police chief, and the head of every law enforcement agency having to do with traffic regulation in the State of Arizona.

The letter reads as follows:

"It has come to my attention that numerous individuals in our state have rescinded all of their contracts with the United States federal government, the State of Arizona, and each of its political subdivisions, establishing themselves as freemen under the organic national Constitution of the Republic of the United States of America. Consequently, they may be driving without auto registration, driver's license, or any other evidence of contract.

"Because many law enforcement personnel may be unaware of the contractual nature of auto registration and driver's licenses, it is conceivable that this situation may lead to confrontation between these individuals and law enforcement personnel.

"I urge you to inform yourself and your personnel about this matter as soon as possible. If you would like to be briefed by someone knowledgeable on this subject, please contact me.

"In the meantime, inasmuch as this procedure is entirely appropriate when properly carried out, I would like to be personally notified of every such instance of confrontation in order that the persons involved and the public officials involved may be apprised of the correct procedure and the appropriateness of their actions on the part of each concerned.

"My office phone is (602) 255-5261 and I am requesting to be notified of the names and incidents along with addresses and phone numbers of participants of any such confrontations arising from the exercise of a person's freeman status in order to evaluate the outcome of properly rescinded contracts.

Sincerely,

Wayne Stump

State Senator

State Capitol - Senate Wing

Phoenix, Arizona 85007

[Reprinted from `Freedom League Newsletter', January 1986]

Big "C" -- Little "c"

When this Nation was founded each of the individual States of this union had their own Citizens (spelled with a capital "C"). Today, we have a second class of citizen (note the small "c"), the 14th Amendment citizen.

In law, **every letter in a word is important.** A word capitalized may mean one specific thing, while the same word without capitalization may mean something entirely different. In the case of Citizenship (or citizenship), this is more certainly true.

There is a clear distinction between **National** and **State** citizenship: *U.S. citizenship does not entitle citizen of the privileges and Immunities of the Citizen of the State. (K. Tashiro v. Jordan, 256 P 545, affirmed 49 S Ct 47, 278 US 123).*

Congress and most of the Judiciary have made rulings based upon the federal "citizens" who are resident in a State, not State Citizens domiciled within their own State, without a proper distinction between the two.

There are two "classes" of citizens in this country:

1. Preamble Citizen: Persons born or naturalized within the meaning of the Organic Constitution and inhabiting one of the several Republics of the United States who enjoy full citizenship of the Organic Constitution as Citizens of the Republic which they inhabit.

2. Citizen "subject": persons enfranchised by the 14th Amendment who are born or naturalized in the United States within the meaning of the 14th Amendment and are residing therein as a United States citizen and are enjoying the privileges and immunities of "limited" citizenship.

When one separates the classes among their appropriate dividing lines, it appears that:

1. Preamble Citizens:
a. Have direct personal access to a God inspired, original Constitution and it's restraints on government for the protection of life, liberty and property.
b. Have direct personal access to the Article III courts known as "justice courts" which deal with law.

2. Citizen "subjects":

a. Have representative access to the first eight amendments as provided by the 14th Amendment. b. Have representative access to Article 1 courts, provided by legislature, that are known as "legislative courts" which deal with statutes and are served by bar members, or officers of the court, known as lawyers.

In many publications, and also personal conversations, people convey their feelings of alarm or despair in finding that "the court" or "government" is in violation of the Constitution without realizing that the court they are addressing **is a legislative court and does not hear cases based on justice, but rather, cases based only on statute law (You are in the wrong court venue).**

The reality of the following example of statute law is that the statute specifies a speed limit to be held at 30 m.p.h. **The only question that can be entertained by the court** is that of *whether the accused did in fact go faster than the limit.* That is a yes or no question. The accused cannot try to tell the court that it was a six-lane highway on a clear day with no traffic in sight and that his speed of 60 m.p.h. did not injure anyone.

The court is not obligated to hear that argument as it is not a justice court. The court that we need to go to **is the article III "justice"(District) court.**

As the truth of our personal status, and the responsibilities connected therewith unfolds, it becomes clear that the Article III "justice" court must be accessed individually by the person claiming the right. At present, it is being done by common law filing of actions "in law" with the County Recorders who have been found to be "ex officio" clerks of the County courts.

Fight your case in the proper venue! It's very Important!!!

"Acts are NOT Laws!"

They know that the public is dumb and are knowingly using "Color of Law" (an act being performed based upon legal right or enforcement of statute, when in reality no such right exists) to assert its will. In other words, they are knowingly holding a colorable posture and are confident that the masses don't know and are only using PUBLIC POLICY not Law to operate on. THERE IS A HUGE DIFFERENCE BETWEEN <u>ACTS</u> AND <u>LAWS</u>! **Acts are NOT Laws! They are only <u>given the force of law</u> when consented by the governed (me and you)! (i.e. Highway Traffic Act)**

First, let's look at a sourced definition of "statute" in which citizens of the UNITED STATES Corporation are governed under.

Statute- An <u>act</u> of the legislature as an organized body. Washington v Dowling, 92 Fla 601, 109 So 588.

inclusive of an **act of the legislature, an administrative regulation**, or an enactment, from whatever source originating, to which the **state gives the force of law**. 50 Am J1st Stat § 2. (Ballantines, 3rd edition, Page 1212)

Let's look at the above phrases "Act of Legislature", "An Administrative Regulation", and "The State"

Act- A thing done or established; a deed or other written instrument evidencing a contract or an obligation. A statute; a bill which has been enacted by the legislature into a law, as distinguished from a bill which is in the form of a law presented to the legislature for enactment. Anne 5 ALR 1422. (Ballantines, 3rd edition, Page 16-17)

Legislature- Broadly, any body having legislative power. 49 Am J1st States § 28. (Ballantines, 3rd edition, Page 724)

Regulation- Control or direction by restriction or rule of something permitted or suffered to exist. 30 Am J rev ed Intox L § 22. Any rule for the ordering of affairs, public or private, whether by statute, ordinance, or resolution. Kepner v Commonwealth, 40 Pa St 124, 129. Ballantines, 3rd edtion, Page 1081)

State-A body politic or society of men united together for the purpose of promoting their mutual safety and advantage by their combined strength, occupying a definite territory, and politically organized under one government. McLaughlin v Poucher, 127 Conn 441, 17

A2d 767. ... a political community of free citizens, occupying a territory of defined boundaries, and organized under a government sanction and limited by a written constitution, **and established by the consent of the governed.** Coyle v Smith, 221 US 559, 55 L Ed 853, 31 S Ct 688. **(Ballantines, 3rd edition, Page 1210)**

Therefore...

An act of the legislature = legislative

An administrative regulation = a rule

The state = a political community, organized under a government, **established by the consent of the governed.**

Connect the dots...As you can see and ACT is only:

A **legislative rule**, ONLY *given the force of law* by the political community that has been established by the **consent** of the governed. DO NOT CONSENT!!!!

As you see by their OWN definition ACTS are NOT LAWS!!!

"Importance of STATUS"

Status is a measure of your legal rank and standing in Society. This involves your capacities and incapacities to exercise and enjoy freedoms and liberties, etc. Therefore, Law, Venue and Jurisdiction are always primal issues to address. Question the authority of those who bring you into a location or 'court". Jurisdiction must be proven for the record and established **before** Adjudication (action and judgment) can be made by the Judge/Jury. Your Status must be 'In Full Life' as opposed to 'Civiliter Mortuus' (dead in the eyes of law...Negro, Black, Colored, ARTIFICIAL PERSON, Latino...etc).

In matters involving Court appearances, hearings, etc., it has already been established that all judicial power is vested in one Court -- the Supreme Court, and to any Courts the Congress may from time to time, delegate such powers to, which is done with a "**Delegation Of Authority Order (DOAO),** and of course it is in written form.

There are three things placed before the Court as a matter of Protocol, prior to Adjudication:

1)Status
2)Jurisdiction/Venue
3)Adjudication

1.Status: (i.e. your social standing in the community; are you a flesh and blood being - a Natural Person, Nationality, or a Corporate Person, an artificial construct). Don't allow them to gain jurisdiction over your Natural person by stating for the record that you are the Natural person, putting your Nationality on record, and claiming Common law jurisdiction.

2. Jurisdiction / Venue: There are three parts of jurisdiction and they **ALL** must be proved in order for the court to adjudicate (rule) in your case.

- A. **Subject Matter Jurisdiction** (Jurisdiction over the Subject Matter)
    - The courts have to have jurisdiction over the actual subject matter.

- B. **In Personam Jurisdiction** (Jurisdiction over the Person)
    - They DO NOT have jurisdiction over your Natural Person only your ARTIFICIAL PERSON.
    - They do not have jurisdiction over National Citizens (Indigenous Citizens).

- C. **Venue Jurisdiction** (Jurisdiction over the Territory)
    - The courts need to have jurisdiction over the actual territory

If you let them get pass on Status, and you let them pass on Jurisdiction / Venue, then the court automatically moves to:

3. Adjudication: (Which is the determination of penalties, punishment, sentencing, including court fees and fines).

Also, when you are dealing with the "Courts", you must ask for their Delegation of Authority Order (DOAO) in written form to be placed on the record, for the record and entered into the record as evidence, as proof of their Authority. It they do not produce it, they don't have it, and technically the matter is closed. **"Ask and you shall receive"**.

You can, and ought to **"Ask"** (and you must be answered) for their Delegation of Authority, particularly and especially in lieu of the fact that most of the Courts, or Tribunals you encounter are Ministerial, and/or Inferior, lacking jurisdiction and lacking Judicial Authority.

You also ask for the Judge/Magistrates' "Oath of Office" *(which indicates their agreement, responsibility, and obligation, taken under* **oath to support the Constitution**, *as the constitution is where their Authority is derived)*. If they give you the run around in regards to acquiring this Oath, which is public information, you can stop the chasing and ask for it.

It is best if you ask for the Oath of Office, and for the DOAO, in a **"Writ of Discovery"** (along with any other requests for information), before you get to court to be prepared (or, you can ask for the DOAO independently...which is best). This request is called an **"Averment of Jurisdiction"**.

If a positive legal Status is not the standing of the 'natural person' before a court, or if it is waived or abandoned, one may be classified 'Civiliter Mortuus'. Whenever one is called before, or enters a court, and one is presented in a 'Pro Se' status, and not as a natural person, (In Propria Persona), one is considered as being in a negative status. If one hires a Lawyer or an Attorney of the Bar Association (A.B.A.) to 're-present' you, then you have surrendered your Birthrights to that officer of the court! Jurisdiction is then assumed, and the officers of the court go straight to Adjudicating against you with sanctions, fines, and jail time, or both! Lawyers and Attorneys are Officers of the Court, and this relationship (of pretended fairness) constitutes a conflict of interest! 'Represent' means, "to appear in the character of; to exhibit; and to expose before the eyes." To represent a person is to supply his place, to act as his substitute; to depict; to mock; to imitate; to act in the character of, etc.

These legal words, terms, and phrases (as noted beneath the scales) are of extreme importance, as they pertain to, and affect, the first judicial issue at law — your Status! One who is in one's own "Proper Person" Status (In Propria Persona), would never utilize, accept, operate, or allow anyone to designate or to refer to them in any of the many 'colored' or improper legal terms, as listed under "Status: Negative" .

Special Appearance vs. Appearance

In Proper Person vs. Pro Se

In Full Life vs. Civiliter Mortuus

Consul vs. Counsel (Attorney)

Natural Person vs. Artificial (Corporate) Person

Sui Juris vs. Minority

Allodial vs. Feudal

We will review each of these 'legal terms' with you, but you are encouraged to take the time to look them up, and to define them etymologically, during your academic studies, and on your own time. We suggest that you use an early—edition Law Dictionary as a general rule. When you compare the earlier editions of Dictionaries with the newer editions, you will see the intellectually conflicting issues for yourselves, as the late editions will be heavily abridged, and void of clarity and depth. As you recognize the deliberate reductions made against exposing knowledge and information, you will willingly and wisely make the necessary connections and study changes with yourselves and within yourselves. It will(immediately) become apparent to you why Scholars and Humanists prize older volumes of Dictionaries and other serious cultural literature. Remember to study for yourselves. Seek and you will find.

"Man knows not by being told" —Prophet Noble Drew Ali

We must never lose focus of the fact that the Judges of all the States, the Administrative Officers of the Courts, and the Politicians, all take their solemn, 'Official Oaths of Office' on the Constitution for the United States of America (the Republic). **That contractual Oath is not to be superseded by police policy code books, nor to be used for revenue extortion schemes, veiled in opportunistic Municipal Rules and Regulations. The Judges' first solemn Obligation is to 'Uphold' the "Supreme Law of the Land" (Constitution).** These Judicators and the Officers of the Courts are 'Bound' by Law, and are 'Authorized' to see that the Law (Constitution) is 'Supported', 'Upheld', and 'Enforced' in all controversies in which the United States, or any of the several States, in the Union, are a party. Judges must be fair and impartial to the Parties before the Courts. **Judges are not Prosecutors**, and violate the Law if they act as Prosecutors, and practice Law from the bench. Judges hold limited authorized positions (being Referees). Law only holds for them to hear and to decide Civil and Criminal Cases brought into their assigned jurisdictional venues and Courts of Law. **Jurisdiction** and **Venue** are limiting aspects of their Authority.

Study these words and analyze their relationships to all parties involved. Study the positive and the negative. Measure your studies with the conceptual understanding received by your familiarity with them:

1. In Propria Persona: In one's own proper person. It was formerly a rule in pleading that pleas to the jurisdiction of the court must be plead 'In Propria Persona' because if pleaded by an attorney they admit the jurisdiction, as an attorney is an officer of the court, and he is presumed to plead after having obtained leave, which admits the jurisdiction.

2. Appearance: In law practice, 'Appearance' means "coming into a court as a party to a suit whether as a Plaintiff or as a Defendant" (to appear is to admit their jurisdiction over you).

3. Sui Juris: means, "of one's own right; possessing full social and civil rights; and not under any legal disability, or under the power of another; nor under guardianship".

4. Status: is "the standing, the state, or the condition; being a social position". It is the legal relation of an individual to the rest of the community. Status also relates to the rights, the duties, the capacities and the incapacities, which determine a person to a given class. It is the legal, personal relationship, not temporary in its nature, nor terminable at the mere will of the parties, with which third persons and the state are concerned. While the term

implies relation it is not a mere relation, because it also means, estate, since it also signifies the condition or circumstances in which one stands in regard to his property.

5. Jurisdiction: In the most simplistic terms, is to speak, to declare, and to administer 'right law'; and involves the 'Legal Power' and 'Authority' to hear and to decide cases; and this is conjoined with the power to execute the laws and for administering Justice. Jurisdiction is that 'proper –power' and right of exercising authority. Jurisdiction, thusly, also relates to the pre-determined, and rightly - bridled limits within which that power may be exercised. And this same time less spirit of Justice applies, too, with a distinct recognition of a specified law court; and to its charge; and to its assigned station in the civil affairs of men. Herein resides the contemplation to the determination of rightful venue.

6. Treaty: In International Law, is a compact made between two or more independent nations, with a view to the public welfare. This constitutes an agreement, a league, or a 'contract' between two or more nations or sovereigns, and formally signed by commissioners, who have been properly authorized(delegated) and solemnly ratified by the several sovereigns, or by the supreme power of each state.

7. Person: In general usage, person means a human being (i.e. a 'natural person'); though by statute, a 'person' may include a firm, labor organizations, partnerships, associations, **corporations**, legal representatives, trustees, trustees in bankruptcy, or receivers.

8. Title: In the law of persons, is a mark, a style, or a designation; being a distinctive appellation of dignity or distinction.

9. Allodial: means '**free**' and not holding to any lord or superior; and relates to that which is owned without obligation of vassalage or fealty; being the opposite of 'Feudal'. (Allodial Title)

10. In Full Life: means, "Continuing in both physical and civil existence; that is, neither actually dead nor Civiliter Mortuus".

11. Civiliter Mortuus: means, 'Civilly dead'; dead in the view of the law. The condition of one who has lost his civil rights and capacities, and is accounted dead in law. (Negro, Black, Colored, Latino, ARTIFICIAL PERSON...etc)

12. Identity: In the Law of Evidence. Sameness; the fact that a subject, a person, or a thing, before a court, is the same as it is represented, claimed, or charged to be.

13. Court: is an organ of the government, belonging to the 'Judicial Department' and whose function is the application of the Laws to controversies brought before it, and for the public administration of Justice. It is a tribunal, officially assembled under an authority of Law, at the appropriate time and place, for the administering of Justice. The Court is an agency of the sovereign, created by it directly or indirectly, under its authority, consisting of one or more officers, established and maintained for the purpose of hearing and determining

issues of law and fact regarding Legal Rights and alleged violations thereof; and of applying the sanctions of the Law, authorized to exercise it powers in due course of Law at times and places previously determined by lawful authority1. Color: is an appearance, a semblance, or a simulacrum, **as opposed to that which is real**. It is a 'prima facie' or apparent right. Hence, it is a deceptive appearance; a plausible, assumed exterior, concealing a lack of reality; a disguise or a pretext. In pleading, 'Color' is a ground of action admitted to subsist in the opposite party by the pleading of one of the parties to an action, which is set out as to be apparently valid, but which is in reality, legally insufficient.

14. Color-Of-Law: **Is the appearance or semblance without the substance** of legal right. Note: Be aware of the fact that anti-constitutional Judges and their colluding court officers, almost always create colorable 'Straw' conditions and arguments before the courts.

"There is no such thing as a power of inherent Sovereignty in the government of the United States. In this country sovereignty resides in the People, and Congress can exercise no power which they have not, by their Constitution entrusted to it: All else is withheld."
[Juilliard v. Greenman, 110 U.S. 421 (1884)]

If we do not understand the rules of the game that is being played against us and the tactics that are used that keep us in mental, financial and informational slavery, then we can never truly be free!

These 'Straw' - personages and arguments, are oriented methodologies explicated by Colonists, and used for institutionalizing forced servitude and slavery. **The undisclosed "Strawman" was devised for constant and deceptive exploitation of the Natural People.**

Lesson #2:

The Truth about: The Untold History

According to The Declaration of Indigenous Rights, indigenous people are those who embody historical continuity with societies **which existed prior to the conquest and settlement of <u>their</u> territories by Europeans.** *As well as people bought involuntary to the new World.*

It's very important to know the real history, World history, European history and dismiss the black and white game and if you don't you are already caught in the trap! It's all about status! Recognizing what Law is, what it is not, and what brings it about can help you tremendously. If you don't understand the political evolution of how the European Colonists established government here and the interchangeable relationship with the Indigenous people who were already here then you can't fully understand the evolution of Law in this country.

There is two people on this planet and that is Asiatic (Original People) and Occidentals (Hybrid People) and everyone else is a blend of the two. After the Spanish Inquisitions and Christian Crusades, books of the ancient world were burned on a massive scale and hidden in secret lodges and libraries so they could create the state of mind that our people are in today. Moor is short for Moroccan ...Moroccans are decedents of the ancient Moabites which inhabited North Central and South Africa, **across the Atlantic into North Central and South America including Mexico and the adjoining islands.** Believe it or not, the pyramids in the Yucatan Peninsula (Central America) **are older** than the Pyramids in Egypt and **are not** different cultures, but variations of the same culture because the Moorish people were on both sides of the Atlantic. As they fell under the Romans, **legally** they fell under the name **Moors.** That was the **last legal name of the aboriginal indigenous** people **in the Western Hemisphere (See Treaty of Peace and Friendship of 1787).** When dealing with law you have to be in your ***proper status legally*** and that includes your National status...not Negro, Black, Colored, Latino, ARTIFICIAL PERSON, which gives this corporate identity faking as government, jurisdiction.

Moors are the decedents of the ancient Moabites. The true Indigenous Peoples who in habited the Northwest and Southwestern Continents (lands) of Ancient Amexem/Al Moroc, now called the Americas (North, Central, South, and the adjoining Islands.) Through the reconstruction of historical writings (The Dark Period). These peoples and their land have been "RENAMED" or "BRANDED" to confuse the people concerning the true geographical location of their native lands which are under siege (Colonization). Moors are bound to the continents of America by heritage and birthright. Moors are not citizens of the Union States Society but are the PEOPLE of the CONTINENETAL UNITED STATES being part and parcel of the government to which the Union of States are obligated. We are what a lot of people would refer to as De Jure.

One of the most detrimental but most successful plans for world conquest is when the sociologists created the artificiality of Race. <u>The artificiality of race was created by making adjectives (something that describes) into nouns (something that is) in order to divide and conquer the indigenous people of these lands and steal their birthrights and inheritance.</u>

To solve this once and for all…we are ALL one broad extended human family, which is broken down into smaller families called Nationalities. That's it! The Race game was played to divide and conquer by hiding people's true National names (Nationality) and re-branding them as African Americans, Native Americans, Mexicans, Puerto Ricans, Dominicans, Haitians, Jamaicans, Virgin Islanders, Pacific Islanders, Indian, Blacks, Negros, Colored which allowed them to steal their Inherent birthrights. If they got them to believe that they were all different people then it would be easy to divide and conquer them. Anyone with Melanin in their skin here in the Western Hemisphere are considered of **Moor**ish/Moabite/**Moroccan/Al' Moroccan (American)** ancestry. Melanin is what causes the pigmentation in the skin of these darker colored intentionally miss-branded people.

"You are able to break someone consciousness by breaking their history, because if they don't know who they are, then you can TELL them who they are!"

The Moors

The Amurru Washitaw Muurs (Moors) were originally a group of priests from Egypt, also known as the Dogon/Olmecs/Mayans. The term Washitaw is a corruption of Ursahtaw, the father and mothers of the mystics. In Egyptian, Ursahtaw is Urrashet, the winged sun disk, which symbolizes the highest knowledge, the pineal gland being open. Egypt was once the capitol of the world. In fact, the Pharaoh gave the ancient Moabites (Moors) permission to settle Morocco, which is now North Africa. The Moabites migrated to modern-day America, and called her Al Morocco, which is another root for the word, America.

The last of the Al Moroccan government fell in 1956 with the abolishment of the Consular Court when **black people accepted civil rights over their natural rights as natural persons.**

Here is a definition of Consular Court:

*A tribunal convened by public officials who reside in a foreign country to protect the interests of their country for the settlement of civil cases based upon situations that happened in the foreign nation and which is held pursuant to authority granted by treaty. (*The 1787 Morocco Treaty of Peace and Friendship was that treaty.*)*

A consular court exercises criminal jurisdiction in some instances, but its determinations are reviewable by the courts of the home government. The last of the U.S. consular courts of Morocco was abolished in 1956.

The 1787 Morocco Treaty of Peace and Friendship was a means to try to stop all of the fighting over land, so the Moors brought the Europeans to the table to form a peaceful two system government; one for the Moors and one for the Europeans. Evidence of this two-system government can be found on the **back of a one-dollar bill**. Notice the two seals. You see one of a pyramid with an eye above it, which was the Moorish seal, and the other seal is that of an eagle holding 13 arrows, which is the European seal. Another example of this two-system government is the Consular Court, which was the Moorish court system. The last one was abolished in 1956 according to the above definition, and this Consular Court was granted its authority by treaty, that is, the 1787 Morocco Treaty of Peace and Friendship. The Europeans had and still do have their court systems, but it's just their system now.

Empress Verdiacee Tiari Washitaw wrote in her book, "The Return of the Ancient Ones**," that "85% of the (so called) blacks over here in America**

were already here before the slave trade. Only 15% of blacks come from Africa." We all come from Africa but there is a suppressed history of **blacks (Moors) being a global people**.

Pangaea proves that all of the continents were connected, so migration to and from Africa and to other places was simple and easy.

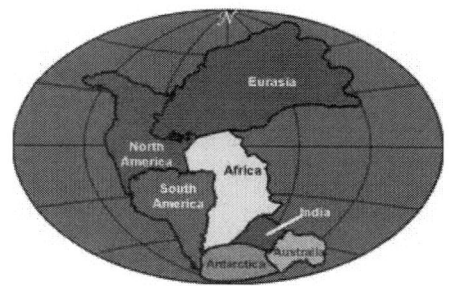

In the book, "America BC," there is an alabaster egg of a cartouche of King Tut found in Idaho. **Africans and Native Americans, by Dr. Jack Forbes, states, "The slave trade started in America and the slaves were taken mostly to Spain and Europe**. When the Spanish came to America they found the Indios (Indians), the people of color who are with God." All of the evidence proves that people of color (Moors) are the oldest natives in America, hands down.

"The African Slave Trade Myth"

Much of the African Slave trade was fabricated and widely exaggerated. In the book *African and Native Americans* by Jack D. Forbes, it says that "The so-called Indians in Terra-Nova (New Land) were Moors." He shows how many so called Native American Indians were sold into slavery in Africa and in Europe. This is the opposite direction in which we were taught the slave trade went! These Native Americans or Indians were classified as Negros and Blacks in the slave books of Seville, Spain and elsewhere. On page 29 he says, "Slaves from Terra-Nova (New World) show up in the slave markets of Seville and Valencia very soon after 1500. For example; in Valencia during the period to 1516 we find in 1503 Miguel Manne, in 1505 Juan and Perdo, in 1507 Antonio and Juan Amarco, in 1515 Ali, now Melchor, in 1516 Catalina…they were ALL classified as Negros…"

Now think about this. If slaves were first brought to North America around 1619 according to school history books then how were they taking slaves from (Tera-Nova) to Europe all before 1520? Keep in mind that one of the Native Americans also had the name ALI, and all were re-classified as Negros once they reached Seville and Valencia. How did a Native American have a Moorish name Ali in 1515? The five Nobel Moorish titles are El, Bey, Dey, Al, and Ali.

At least 3,000 so called Indians are known to have been shipped from America to Europe between 1493 and 1501 called "The Columbus Expeditions." Most show up in the Seville, Spain area where they seem to show up in the slave markets as Negros. Black Moors were ALWAYS in America. The missing Indians everyone has been searching for all this time are the "Negros" that have been misclassified and brainwashed throughout generations.

The Slaves sold here in the south were initially Moors from RIGHT HERE in this hemisphere. It only made sense as they took the land here to enslave the inhabitants of those lands who called themselves Moors before Columbus renamed them "Indians" thinking he had arrived in India. The tens of millions of Americans (so called Indians) didn't all die in the Holocaust here in America, many thousand were shipped to Europe and Africa as slaves. The whole slave trade myth is that the whole story was given to us in reverse! Let me explain.

The whole story is that mass colonies of Africans were not shipped from Africa to America. The truth is that "Black Indians" (Moors) were shipped from America to Europe, then from Spain to Africa as a commodity for African resources. Once the labor pool began to deplete from the Moors (Indians) in America because of death and suicide, the labor was replaced by those "Black Indians" (Moors) in Africa, now misclassified as Negros and began to be shipped back to America.

This part of the history is what the school system failed to mention in their history program!!

The gold and precious metals Columbus excavated from America fueled a 400% inflation that eroded the economies of Non-European Nations and helped Europe create a Global market system. Africa suffered a great economic blow because the Trans-Saharan trade collapsed (Africa's precious jewel and gem trade) because America began supplying more precious metal and gems which almost wiped out Western Africa's global market position. Therefore, African traders only had one commodity that Europe wanted...SLAVES! As a result, African Sultans sold their own people into slavery to

Europeans. It is safe to say that Christopher Columbus is solely responsible for the slavery of the Moors from West to East and East to West.

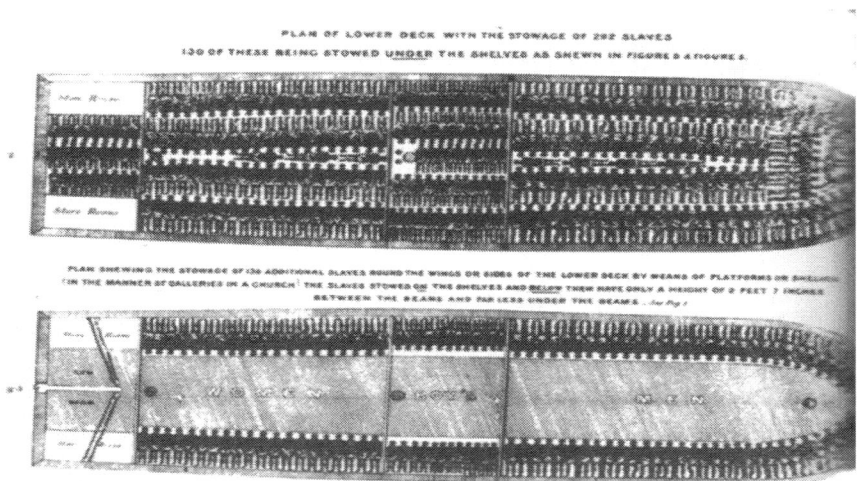

Above is a picture of a "Big Bottom" ship. As you can see this is what was supposed to transport 300 to 400 "African slaves" from Western Africa to the Americas. These trips would have taken 3 to 4 months at a time with the slaves packed head to foot like sardines. It was noted that the slaves urinated and defecated on themselves throughout the voyage. Now come on! Do you really believe that 300 to 400 large bodied people could even survive a 3 to 4-month trip packed like sardines and using the bathroom on each other? They would have literally drowned in their own waste! It just doesn't make sense. We were already here. In Central America, Archaeologists have found multi-ton stone heads which had large noses (a distinctively non-European trait) pre-dating the Great pyramids of Egypt.

THE OLMECS

The first great American civilization was that of the Olmecs of Mexico. From 1200 BC, they developed a highly organized society, centered on spectacular sites built for religious ceremonies at San Lorenzo and La Venta. Olmec people sculpted huge monuments in stone and portable figurines in jade. Many Olmec achievements benefited later American societies, earning Olmec culture the name "mother culture."

COLOSSAL HEAD
Eight giant stone heads were found at San Lorenzo, Mexico. They probably show Olmec rulers.

© Copyright 2001 Artistic Studios Proactive Marketing & Publishers Service
All Rights Reserved

The first known civilization in America (Central America) was called the **Olmec** (Old Mex). The Olmec people built large multi-ton heads with uniquely African features (wide nose, large lips) proving that the first people here in America were distinctively Moorish.

What we see as and call Indians (Native Americans) today are actually descendants of the Olmecs (Moors) mixed with Mongolian.

Why is this Information Suppressed?

Well Europeans want you all to believe that people of color (Moors) only come from Africa to keep the land they have taken and not feel so guilty about it. If you can distort the history of the blood shed for the land, you can appear more humane. That's exactly what they did. They wrote a his-story book after they were firmly established to tell his-story more humanely. The American- His-story book has been a great success because it has most of the world blind as to what really happen. People of color(Moors) are universal, they tried to call us Africans but we are Asiatic, meaning we span and originate from every place on earth (Africa, Asia India, Australia, all the islands, etc), we are the original native Americans.

Ask yourself:

Who was here before 1492?

What was here in operation?

Who were the people?

What kind of systems and Laws did they live by?

Answer: The 'natural people' "The Mud Colored People" who are the Founders of Civilization, and the Mothers and Fathers of the Human Family, were called Moors / Muurs / Mu / Maure / Maurus / More / Moorens / Moroccan / Al Moroccans, etc. These are some of the dialectical pronunciations, according to varied languages, such as, Moorish Latin, Middle English, Germanic, French, Greek, etc.

Who is Original Man and Woman?

Answer: the Ancient Moabites / Muurs / Moors; the Asiatics-sometimes referred to as, Mu, Lemurians; and in latter history, Canaanites / Africans.

Are we All Americans?

Answer: Assuming this question is directed to the dark olive Asiatic Aboriginals of the Land, the response is that the Moors are the true possessors of the present Moroccan Empire, which spans from 'Tamari' (now called Africa), even across the great Atlantis; and includes, Northwest, Central, and Southwest Amexem, and the Atlantis Islands. These geographical areas are now called, America; North, Central, South, and the adjoining Islands.

Who is this Man Amerigo Vespucci, that Europeans claim America was name after?

Answer: Amerigos Vespucius was a European of Italus (Italian) descent; and a neophyte explorer who sailed from the Moorish city of Khadiz (Cadiz), to learn of latitudinal and longitudinal imaginary gridline used by the Moors for navigating the Earth. Particularly using the Sextant to measure one heavenly body in relation to another, against the horizon, for determining longitude and latitude positions while at sea or on the oceans.

What is this name Amexum that The Moors claim the Americas was called?

Answer: Amexem is the ancient name of the lands known as, Including North, Central, and South America.

Who is Christopher Columbus and if he is the One Who Discovered America, why was this continent not named after him?

Answer: Christopher Columbus was a European Inquisitionist, whose actual mission was theft and murder by genocide: initiated for Christendom, against the Aboriginal Moabite /

Moorish tribes of Western Hemisphere. The continent was not named after Columbo because he didn't discovery America. Ameru / America / Amexem already had its name, and was already a highly cultured and thriving Civilization.

Who are the Native Americans?

Answer: 'Native American' is another contemporary sociology term or "**disassociation conquest tag"** (an invented construct of European conquerors). It, like many other misnomers and tags, is not a national identity of the Aboriginals, but is a political status-class designation, designed to expand upon social and political divisions, displacement, and confusion amongst the Aboriginal Moors of the Americas.

Are We Black, Brown, Red, Yellow, White people?

Answer: No, Asiatics are not Black, Brown, Red, Yellow, Orange, Light-skinned black, purple, Plaid, or Green people, etc. The Human Family (collectively) is identified and known by **'Nationalities'** and pedigree names-not by crayon colors. This deep sign of mental ignorance was promoted by Inquisitionists to **denationalize** the rightful Heirs and Inheritors of the Land (America / Al Moroc). However, the Europeans were calling themselves 'Red Men' prior to the political adaptation of the political status, 'White men" in the 1854-63. This caste adaptation was initiated by Horace Greeley, a newspaper tycoon from New York. He influenced the transformation of the 'Whiggamore (Whigs) party' into the 'Republican party' during the establishment of the Knights of Columbus and Ku Klux Klan Oath of 1854 to 1863, in Philadelphia, Pennsylvania, and Chicago, Illinois, United States of North America. It must be further understood that the term, **"Free White Person"**

is a **social caste** appellation in Jurisprudence, and **nothing to do with complexion of skin.**

"FREE WHITE PERSONS"

> **FREE WHITE PERSONS.** "Free white persons" referred to in Naturalization Act, as amended by Act July 14, 1870, has meaning naturally given to it when first used in 1 Stat. 103, c. 3, meaning all persons belonging to the European races then commonly counted as white, and their descendants, including such descendants in other countries to which they have emigrated.
>
> It includes all European Jews, more or less intermixed with peoples of Celtic, Scandinavian, Teutonic, Iberian, Latin, Greek, and Slavic descent. It includes Magyars, Lapps, and Finns, and the Basques and Albanians. It includes the mixed Latin, Celtic-Iberian, and Moorish inhabitants of Spain and Portugal, the mixed Greek, Latin, Phoenician, and North African inhabitants of Sicily, and the mixed Slav and Tarter inhabitants of South Russia. It does not mean Caucasian race, Aryan race, or Indo-European races, nor the mixed Indo-European, Dravidian, Semitic and Mongolian peoples who inhabit Persia. A Syrian of Asiatic birth and descent will not be entitled to become a naturalized citizen of the United States as being a free white person. Ex parte Shahid, D.C.S.C., 205 F. 812, 813; United States v. Cartozian, D.C.Or., 6 F.2d 919, 921; Ex parte Dow, D.C.S.C., 211 F. 486, 487; In re Sk Song, D.C.Cal., 271 F. 23. Nor a native-born Filipino. U. S. v. Javier, 22 F.2d 879, 880, 57 App.D.C. 303. Nor a native of India who belonged to Hindu race. Kharaiti Ram Samras v. United States, C.C.A.Cal., 125 F.2d 879, 880.

As you see above, **Free White Person** includes- "...**Moorish** ...and exclusively says...**Does not mean** Caucasian race, Aryan race, or Indo-European races, nor the mixed Indo-European, Dravidian Semetic or Asiatic birth

and descent will not be entitled to become a naturalized citizen of the United States." – **Blacks Law Dictionary 4th edition**

The phrase "White" people has NOTHING to do with skin complexion and everything to do with STATUS! This caste adaptation was initiated by Horace Greeley, a newspaper tycoon from New York. The "White" cast was adopted/stolen by the Whiggamore party (now known as the Republican Party) in Philadelphia, Pennsylvania between 1852 and 1863. What did they call themselves before then you ask? They called themselves REDmen. The term "White" is an ancient caste STATUS term, which applies to status and not to complexion of skin. The artificiality of race was created by making adjectives (something that describes) into nouns (something that is) in order to divide and conquer the indigenous people of these lands and steal their birthrights and inheritance.

Did you know that **the family of nations WILL NOT recognize you as a member of the human race if you do not have a NATIONALITY and that you are considered a refugee** [see U.S immigration & nationality act, section101(a)(42) & section 207(e)] remember black is a color not a nation. Even though Europeans call themselves white, if you ask them their nationality they'll will tell you Irish, German, Scottish, Dutch etc. If people ask most "black people" today they say that they are **African American**, but **Africa is not a country it is a continent** with over 50 countries in it. America isn't just specific to North America, **there are 3 Americas, North, Central &South,**

with many countries encompassed within it as well. The term African American doesn't Identify with any specific geographical location (i.e. Nation) in the human family.

The Moors Sundry Act of 1790

The Moors Sundry Act of 1790 was passed by South Carolina legislature, granting special status to the subjects of Sultan of Morocco, Mohammed ben Abdallah. It recognized Moors as **"white"** people with Jury duty as a privilege. Moors were not to be subjected to laws governing Blacks and slaves.

On January 20, 1790, a petition was presented to the South Carolina House of Representatives from a group of eight individuals who were subjects of the Moroccan emperor and residents of the colony. They desired that if they happened to commit any fault amenable to be brought to justice, that as subjects to a prince allied with the United States through the Moroccan-American Treaty of Friendship, they would be tried as citizens instead of under the Negro Act.

The Free Moors, Francis, Daniel, Hammond and Samuel petitioned on behalf of themselves and their wives Fatima, Flora, Sarah and Clarinda. They explained how some years ago while fighting in defense of their country, they and their wives were captured and made prisoners of war by the Portuguese. After this a certain Captain Clark had them delivered to him, promising they would be redeemed by the Moroccan ambassador residing in England, and returned to their country. Instead, he transported them to South Carolina, and sold them for slaves. Since then, "by the greatest industry," they purchased freedom from their respective masters: They requested that as free born subjects of a Prince in alliance with the U.S., that they should not be considered subject to a State Law (then in force) known as the negro law. If they be found guilty of any crime or misdemeanor, they would receive a fair trial by lawful jury. The matter was referred to a committee consisting of Justice Grimke, General Charles Pinckney and Edward Rutledge.

Free Moors Petition: Ruling

Edward Rutledge reported from the committee referred to the Free Moors petition. The order for immediate consideration of the matter was read and agreed to as follows "They have Considered the same and are of opinion that no Law of this State can in its Construction or Operation apply to them, and that **persons who were Subjects of the Emperor of Morocco being Free in this State are not triable by the Law for the better Ordering and Governing of Negroes and other Slaves."**

Again, those who REMEMBERED that they were Moors used the Free MOOR SUNDRY ACT and the MOROCCAN TREATY OF PEACE AND FRIENDSHIP to **secure their status**. Those who were brainwashed into thinking they were Negros,

Descendants of Africans brought by Europeans WERE NOT protected by the Moroccan Treaty, Articles of Confederation or the Constitution.

"Honor your father and mother" - *Ephesians 6:2*

According to The Declaration of Indigenous Rights, indigenous people are those who embody historical continuity with societies which existed prior to the conquest and settlement of their territories by Europeans. As well as people bought involuntary to the new World. (See http://bit.ly/cJpHi4)

According to the above United Nations treaty, all "black" people are indigenous. This means that Blacks are natural persons. All natural persons are human beings and sovereigns of the land, because they rightfully own the land. This is coming from the Black's Law Dictionary. Just look up natural persons. All blacks are beyond first-class citizens and don't even know it, because we have accepted His-story and slave labels like, negro, black, and colored.

What makes the above treaty so powerful is that according to Article VI of the United States Constitution, **"Treaties are the Supreme law of the land."** The United States of America is a part of the United Nations, so the Government is bound by it.

Sovereignty resides in your Nationality. Your Nationality ties you back to the land. What is your Nationality? My Nationality is Moorish.

The washitaw tribal Moors are listed at the United Nations under the Indigenous People Organization Number 21593. This became effective in 1993. The seat number for the Washitaw at the United Nations is 215.

According to International Law, the Washitaw has established itself as a Sovereign Independent Nation (United Nations, NIS-21/593) apart from corporate union of 1781 and the corporate United States of 1787. The land claim of the Washitaw has been affirmed by the Spanish and French, as well as British, pursuant to Spanish Land Grants of 1762 and 1795.

According to Federal Law, the land of the Washitaw has been defined as "Indian Country," and the people regarded as Indians. Both the people and their land have been placed under the authority of the United States government via the Bureau of Indian Affairs within the Department of Interior, which is governed by both Executive and Congressional Plenary powers. As a result, the United states has assumed the "Trust responsibility" for the Washitaw Nation of Muurs (Moors) via Spanish Land Grant of Henry Turner.

"UNIVERSAL DECLARATION OF HUMAN RIGHTS"
Adopted and proclaimed by the General Assembly resolution 217 A (III) of December 1948

Article 15.
(1) Everyone has the right to a nationality.
(2) No one shall be arbitrarily deprived of his nationality nor denied the right to change his nationality.

Excerpts from the **UNITED NATIONS DECLARATIONS ON THE RIGHTS OF INDIGENOUS PEOPLES**
The General Assembly, Taking note of the recommendation of the Human Rights Council contained in its resolution 1/2 of 29 June 2006, by which the Council adopted the text of the United Nations Declaration on the Rights of Indigenous Peoples, Distr.: Limited 7 September 2007 Passed 13 September 2007

Article 2
Indigenous peoples and individuals are free and equal to all other peoples and individuals and have the right to be **free from any kind of discrimination**, in the exercise of their rights, in particular that based on their indigenous origin or identity.

Article 4
Indigenous peoples, in exercising their right to self-determination, have the **right to autonomy or self-government** in matters relating to their internal and local affairs, as well as ways and means for financing their autonomous functions.

Article 6
Every indigenous individual has the right to a nationality.

Article 8
1. Indigenous peoples and individuals have the right not to be subjected to forced assimilation or destruction of their culture.
2. States shall provide effective mechanisms for prevention of, and redress for:
(a) Any action which has the aim or effect of depriving them of their integrity as distinct peoples, or of their cultural values or ethnic identities;
(b) Any action which has the aim or effect of dispossessing them of their lands, territories or resources;
(c) Any form of forced population transfer which has the aim or effect of violating or undermining any of their rights;
(d) Any form of forced assimilation or integration;
(e) Any form of propaganda designed to promote or incite racial or ethnic discrimination directed against them.

Article 9
Indigenous peoples and individuals have the **right to belong to an indigenous community or nation, in accordance with the traditions and customs of the community or nation concerned.** No discrimination of any kind may arise from the exercise of such a right.

Article 13
1. Indigenous peoples have the right to revitalize, use, develop and transmit to future generations their histories, languages, oral traditions, philosophies, writing systems and literatures, and to **designate and retain their own names for communities, places and persons.**
2. States shall take effective measures to ensure that this right is protected and also to ensure that indigenous peoples can understand and be understood in political, legal and administrative proceedings, where necessary through the provision of interpretation or by other appropriate means.

You MUST know that there are four classifications of Citizenship (From Highest Status to Lowest Status)!

1. National Citizen

2. Political citizen (US Citizen)

3. Subject

4. Alien

National Citizen- The highest status in any country. A National citizen is a citizen who is attached to the land by birthright and bloodline and would be considered Indigenous. These people have natural born rights given to them by their creator that cannot be infringed upon with manmade statues, codes, ordinances, etc. These people abide by Common Law, the Constitution and treaties, not by the millions of statues made to infringe on the people and steal their resources.

Political citizen (US citizen)- Second highest status in any country. This is the status that most people in America have today. These citizens have agreed (either knowingly or unknowingly) to the statues, regulations, and policies of the corporation of the UINITED STATES or their respective country. These citizens are given a birth certificate with an ALL CAPITAL letters name that looks just like theirs but are really a corporate identity (corporation made to look like your name). These citizens natural born rights are taken away and in return are given "privileges".

Subject/Ward of State- These people are people who reside in a country but have no rights.

Alien- This is the lowest status in any country. This is someone who is from one country but resides in another "illegally".

If one doesn't understand the different classifications of citizenship then one tends to operate in other jurisdictions and in their own community not understanding their legal status. And STATUS IS THE FIRST ISSUE AT LAW!!! Because that determines your capacities and incapacities of operations of dealings with rights, recourses, legal matters in society. Status, Jurisdiction, Adjudication...These things are convoluted with us because we don't' know civics.

The first issue at law that comes before any lawful court is status/Nationality. For Example, it is important for Indigenous people of this land to let the courts know their National Citizen status and at that moment the courts will not have jurisdiction over them. On the other hand, if they did not put their Nationality on record then they would be fined, imprisoned and treated just as the other STRAWMEN and women have been for all of these years.

"The Period of Reconstruction"

The Moroccan Treaty of Peace and Friendship allowed the Europeans to do Commerce in this Moorish Empire in a ten by ten square mile designated area which is now call Washington D.C. In an attempt to expand their territory and power some Europeans have and are still trying to overthrow the Treaty and De Jure Government that was already established in this land as the true Republic. When children say the National anthem "...and to the REPUBLIC for which it stands...", that is exactly what they are talking about.

The Europeans began to overthrow it by attempting to steal the Nationality and birth rights from the Moors by rebranding them Negro, Black and Colored. Then as of, 1779 they retroactively (meaning went back after the fact) added the Nergo, Black and Colored brand/label into the history books, also began burning books (Look up the Christian Book Burnings), burning documents, moving documents and books to secret lodges (Masonic Lodges), making new records and listing the Moors as Black, Negro and Colored. They would move the children from the southeast to the north west, and the children from the northeast to the southwest, and so on in order to separate the sons from the mothers which would also separate the family from its heritage because the women held the principals of civilization. The evidence of Moorish Heritage in THIS land was supposed to be hidden for 300 to 1000 years, and that accepted social construct is REALLY what the "Period of Reconstruction" was ALL about in the United States.

People are wrongly under the impression that Columbus and the Inquisitionists established government and the United States. Wrong! The United States already existed. The United States was a United Coalition of Moorish tribes that they mistakenly called

"Indians." On my Father's side of the family is what they call Black Foot and on my Mother's side is what they call Cherokee…and **I'm not Indian**. The word Indian is a BRAND. Some tribes sold out but most didn't, which didn't constitute an agreement with the entire Nation although the government will say it did. That's why they had to murder so many of them and separate the mothers who carried the principals of civilization from the children.

<u>One of the commitments of the Inquisitionists was to wipe the Moorish Heritage in this land out of history. That's why it is very hard to find a linear history when it pertains to people of color in the Western hemisphere. But that is also why you have all these secret societies that consequently and curiously inside their lodges KEEP wearing the Moorish fez (head dress).</u> But you never figured it out! They know who the Moors are, but don't want us to know because "Knowledge is Power." <u>They'll have badges on their cars and hats with the Moorish star, or the Eastern star that say, Medina, Morocco, and El (Noble Title), Bey (Noble Title), on the head dresses and badges. They name all their Masonic lodges after women (the mother) because the Moors used to have a Matriarchal society. Then they re-write the history and tell us that we came from someplace else (To steal our Birthrights/Nationality)</u>!

The world knows EXACTLY who the Moors are, and are waiting for them to awaken. In Secret Their existence is ritualized by those who sit in the seats of Power, who have adopted their information, and wear THEIR Noble Titles, as shown in these above photos. Written right on their Fez (Hats). **Top Left:** Islam; **Top Right**: Moslem; **Bottom Left**: El, Bey; **Bottom Right:** Morocco. These photos are from the George Washington Masonic Lodge! Masonry is an open secret of who the Moors are!

One of the keys here also is that they can't deport the Moors to anywhere, that's why they have to keep building jails. Also, contrary to popular belief, the stars and stripes flag (red, white, and blue) does not identify with any blood line or any Native people. It is only a representation of an agreement between the Moorish Nation that was already here and the Inquisitionist that wanted to operate in commerce in this land (Moroccan Treaty of Peace and Friendship of 1787). Our public schools have done an intentional dumb down of information to keep us where we are at. For example, if you ask a child to point to America on the map the child will only point at North America. What they failed to realize is that America includes South, Central, and North America. Who is the American President? Barack Obama? No. He is not the President of Brazil, or the president of Mexico. But there is a United States of Central America, and United States of Brazil but we were never taught this. The term "United States" is only a generic term. There is no such thing as THE American President! There are many American President<u>s</u> and there are many American Flag<u>s</u> from Alaska to Brazil and all the adjoining Islands. The stars and stripes flag is not a flag of any native people it arose from treaties of commerce. The continental flag of the people is a red flag with a cherry tree **(George Washington's "Chopping down the cherry tree")**

What really shook up and scared the secret societies and the elite ruling class of Europeans is when in 1913 Noble Dru Ali began issuing Nationality cards to the Indigenous people. What that began to establish is the true sovereign and true jurisdiction of this land. Just as if I were to go to Russia and try to start arguing Law they would first ask for my Nationality card to check my status to see if I was even allowed to argue Law in their Jurisdiction. You can be a Natural citizen (Moor)/Natural Person of the land, or you can be a Political citizen of an organized government. Both of which require proof!

People's concept of what slavery is in the Western Hemisphere is all wrong, because the government and policy makers are instituting and maintaining slavery **bureaucratically** now **not physically**. Their tactics have changed but we haven't learned or even been aware of what's going on and how to protect ourselves. I hope by a further reading of this book you will begin to open your eyes and begin to ask questions.

Politicians, some of whom were former slaveholders at that time, created a **fraudulent** court called Admiralty court (Traffic Court) and listed it under **crimes**, (because the Constitution only allows two courts, the Criminal and Civil court). You can't try a Criminal case in Civil court and you can't try a Civil case in Criminal court. So where did the Constitution set up traffic court to stop the people from freedom of passage over the land? Nowhere! **The elements of a crime are harm, injury, or loss**, and if these prerequisites are not met then lawfully there is no crime. They prey upon our ignorance of the law in order to steal our money and control the masses. For example, all they have to do to break up your home is put an officer on your street corner and have him keep stopping you which would result in him taking your license from you, therefore, causing you to no longer to be able to make a living! These are private corporate entities operating on a private charter, working with the policy makers to interfere with the rights of the Citizens and the Natural people. These corporations are robbing us legally…not lawfully, there is a big difference!

People who consider themselves to be Negros, Blacks, Colored, African American, Latino, cannot represent themselves at law because they are considered CIVILITER MORTUUS which means dead in the eyes of the law (one who is considered as if he were naturally dead, so far as his rights are concerned). This is because nowhere in Law and nowhere on this planet is there a Nationality called Negro, Black, or Colored, or Latino, it doesn't exist (They are only brand names not Nationalities). But if you agree to be something that someone else created to name their chattel, (NBC-Negro, Black and Colored) it's your fault not theirs for your lack of knowledge. If you agree to be what they rebranded you to be then true Law does not apply to you because there is no such thing as Negro, Black, or Colored in the Human family and the Law only applies to natural humans. As a consequence, you have been subjected to the Christian Black Codes of 1724 which was implemented to govern such people who didn't know who they were. This is the reason they want to hide the Moorish connection because the United States Republic came out of the dissolution of the Moroccan (AL 'Moroccan) Government HERE in this land (The United States of AL' Morocco).

The Europeans were not Indigenous to this land and did not have jurisdiction here so they ended up bringing the Law of the seas (Admiralty and Maritime) onto the land and we didn't even debate it! We just started assuming that they had jurisdiction, and they assumed the jurisdiction that we gave them. This was the BIGGEST mistake and is what secured the very corruption that I'm talking about. They superimposed the Law of the Seas (Admiralty and Maritime) on top of the Law of the land (Common Law) as evidenced by the yellow fringe around the flag that you see in every courtroom or office of government. That's why it is so important to understand and declare your Nationality because it begins to establish the truth about jurisdiction. WE never questioned them and they became secure! We became secure in the corruption of fiction, artificial persons, fiction of brand names and the fiction of inferiority while they became secure in a position of sovereign superiority and authority.

The COLONIZERS use deceit by way of semantics and word play such as "residence", "mail", "US citizen", "last name", and fictional regions "FL", "PA", "CA", "TX" in order to expand their control and got us to agree because our "silence is acquiescence", or "you agree by being silent" and not challenging what happened. They also got us to agree to their other instruments that secure their jurisdiction over us such as the birth certificate, driver's license and social numbers. What we need to understand is the UNITED STATES does not have lawful jurisdiction outside of Washington D.C., Guam, Puerto Rico, U.S. Virgin Islands, and a few military bases.

"The laws of Congress with respect to those matters DO NOT EXTEND into the territorial limits of the STATES, but have force ONLY in the District of Columbia, and places that are within the jurisdiction of the national government..." - Caha vs. the U.S.

"THE UNITED STATES IS A FOREIGN CORPORATION WITH RESPECT TO THE STATE (PEOPLE)" – Vol 20: Corpus Juris Sect 1785

Blacks Law dictionary 5th edition states "A democracy is that form of government in which the sovereignty resides in as is exercised by the whole body of FREE CITIZENS directly or indirectly through a system of representation." Simply stated, a democracy is the dictatorship of the MAJORITY over the MINORITY i.e. negros, blacks, coloreds, African American, Latinos, Hispanics, etc. In a democracy, the minority has no rights; only **privileges** granted by a condescending majority. These privileges are called **Civil Rights.**

"**A minority is one who is stateless**" Nationality Act Sec 101(a) (42) and Sec 207(e). Without a NATIONALITY, you are considered a refugee.

Negros, Blacks, Coloreds, African-American, Indian, Hispanic and Latino are all considered MINORITIES. **A MINORITY/MINOR DOES NOT MEAN WHAT YOU THINK!!!** *A minor/minority is one who does not comprehend what is happening to him/her when a legal matter is being presented. A minority is one who doesn't know their true proper National status (not Negro, Black, Colored, Latino). A minor/minority is one who is incapable of presenting him or herself* therefore, needs to be re-presented by a pro-se cutor.

Part 1 article 5 of the "Declaration of the Rights of Indigenous People" states "Every Indigenous person has a right to a NATIONALITY." **Under the 14th amendment your RIGHTS are taken and in return you are given PRIVILEDGES. HOWEVER, you must AGREE to be negro, black, colored, African American, Latino, Hispanics, etc.** One agrees by accepting instruments of incorporation such as the birth certificate, driver's license, marriage license and social security card which are all unconstitutional and not challenging the brand by correcting your status. Once you learn about and begin to honor your ancestors by recognizing your true free national name (Honor thy mother and father) then the jurisdiction of the UNITED STATES corporation is no longer applicable to you.

"They have considered the same and are of opinion that **NO LAW OF THIS STATE CAN IN ITS CONSTRUCTION APPLY TO THEM** and that persons who WERE Subjects of the EMPEROR of MOROCCO being FREE in this state (here in America) ARE NOT TRIABLE by the laws for better ordering of the Negros..." –MOORS SUNDRY ACT of 1790

"Act Aug 1st, 1956 REEALED sections 141-143 effective upon the date which the President determined to be appropriate for the **RELINQUISHMENT OF JURISDICTION OF THE UNITED STATES IN MOROCCO.** Jurisdiction of Morocco was relinquished by memorandum of President Eisenhower on September 15th 1960. (United States Code Tittle 22 Chapter 2 Section 141-143)

People are not crayons! People have Nationalities!!! Moors gave up their birthright when they accepted being branded Negro, Black and Colored, gave up their culture, fell into servitude, and have been transacting business in alien names for generations...all the while thinking that they were secure.

Article 15 of the Universal Declaration of Human Rights states:

- (1) **Everyone has the right to a nationality.**
- (2) **No one shall be arbitrarily deprived of his nationality nor denied the right to change his nationality.**

If you create a name or brand that was not, (Artificial Person, Negro, Black, Colored) then the law applies to that which you regulate in that jurisdiction. Once you get someone to agree to be in that jurisdiction or be what they are not then…you got them! This is what happened to us, we agreed to be something we were not and under a jurisdiction that we did not have to be subject to because we agreed to be the name and brand that they created. But we had to do it willingly because everything in civilization operates on contract. That's why in court proceedings they ask you "Do you understand?" What they really mean is do you agree because they cannot proceed until they have your consent.

The following are actual photos of European men who wear the Fez behind closed doors (clandestine) in secret societies wherein they perform rituals, take oaths to demi-gods and work hard to keep the Light of Truth regarding the North Gate (North America / Northwest Amexem / Northwest Africa) closed to the masses, even unto the Mothers and Fathers of Civilization, who in fact taught them (Europeans) and brought them out of the Dark Ages during the European Renaissance. They taught through Masonic orders (Ma and Son), the science of the universe, the sacred lessons of life and nature, in an effort to civilize them and bring them into culturized society. The Europeans later created Clandestine orders to keep the teachings amongst themselves.

What we especially want to show in these photo is that not only are they wearing the Fez, written atop them are **Islam, El Bey, Moslem and Morocco,** to show they in fact are aware of Morocco (the Empire and the subordinate kingdom), they are aware and practice Islam and know the true meaning of Moslem, and they are aware of the 5 Noble Titles: El, Bey, Dey, Al, and Ali. These titles were transferred and re-named as the 5 Civilized tribes of acceptance during the so-called "Indian" agreements. However, many are aware now that this is not India, the people were / are Indigenous (Indigenes).

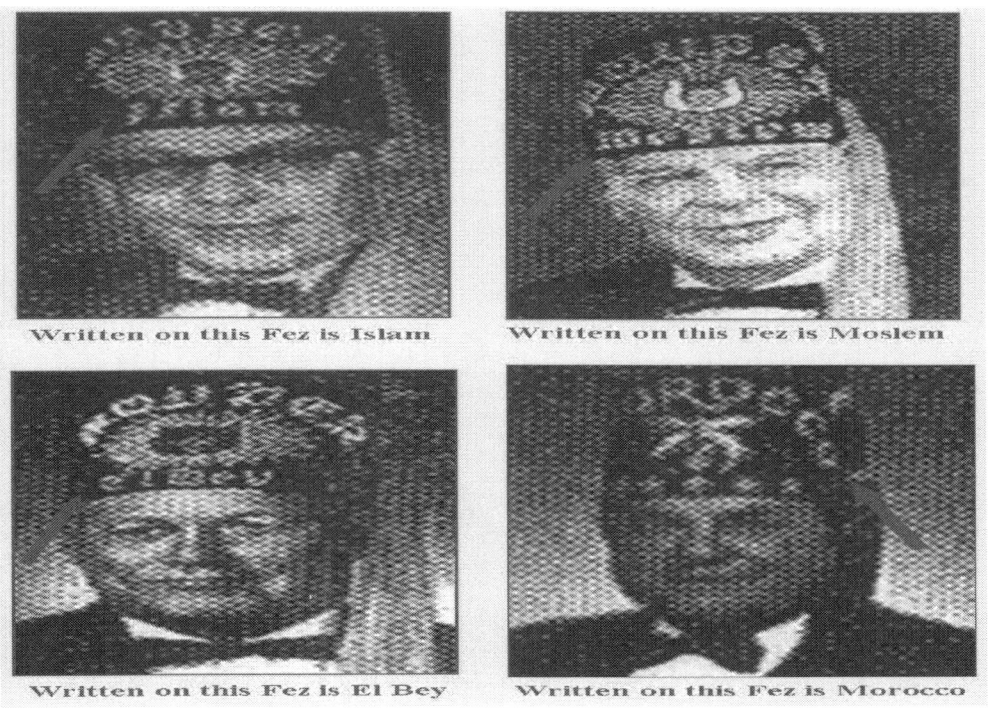

Written on this Fez is Islam   Written on this Fez is Moslem

Written on this Fez is El Bey   Written on this Fez is Morocco

<u>**The world knows EXACTLY who the Moors are**</u>, and are waiting for them to awaken. In Secret, their existence is ritualized by those who sit in the seats of power, who have adopted their information, and wear THEIR Noble Titles, as shown in these above

photos. Written right on their Fez (Hats). **Top Left:** Islam; **Top Right**: Moslem; **Bottom Left**: El, Bey; **Bottom Right:** Morocco. These photos are from the George Washington Masonic Lodge!

"Malcolm X found out he was a MOOR"

We all know the story of Malcolm X but it was never fully explained...

Malcolm grew up as Malcolm Little the later put and X in place of his last name Little because obviously he was not honoring his foremothers and forefathers by wearing a European tittle as a last name. After the death of the Moorish Science Temple leader Noble Drew Ali the Nation of Islam was formed by a former high-ranking member who wanted to take over the Moorish Science Temple but was not allowed named Walter Faroque. He was succeeded by Elijah Muhammad, who was succeeded by who you know today as Minister Louis Farrakhan. The Nation of Islam was on the right track but did not take it all the way home. They told him who he wasn't (Little...European title) and replaced it with an X but failed to tell him who he was politically, historically, legally and status wise! We have all heard the story about Malcolm taking his pilgrimage to Mecca and when he got there he found out that he was mistakenly under the impression that he was making a pilgrimage home, when the biggest revelation he ever got was revealed to him, "YOU WERE ALREADY HOME...YOU LEFT HOME." What he found out is that the North Gate (North America) was actually his home by birthright and heritage! Not so-called Africa or Mecca.

When Malcolm returned and found out the truth about who he was as a Moorish American he then corrected his name and added Moorish Titles to his name. He corrected his name to be El-Hajj Malik El-Shabazz. El is one of the five noble Moorish titles and further adds proof of his new found understanding of who he was and who we are today. As a result of knowing this information...He was shortly thereafter assassinated.

Below is a quote from one of his early interviews:

MALCOLM X: "Well, Hannibal, the most successful general that ever lived, was a black man. So was Beethoven; Beethoven's father was one of the blackamoors that hired themselves out in Europe as professional soldiers. Haydn, Beethoven's teacher, was of African descent. And Solomon. Great Biblical characters. Columbus, the discoverer of America, was a half-black man. Whole black empires**, like the Moorish, have been whitened to hide the fact that a great black empire had conquered a white empire even before America was discovered. The Moorish civilization--black Africans--conquered and ruled Spain; they kept the light burning in Southern Europe. The word "Moor" means "black," by the way.** Egyptian civilization is a classic example of how the white man stole great African cultures and makes them appear today as white European. The black nation of Egypt is the only country that has a science named after its culture: Egyptology. The ancient Sumerians, a black-skinned people, occupied the Middle Eastern areas and were contemporary with the Egyptian civilization. The Incas, the Aztecs, the Mayans, all dark-skinned Indian people, had a highly developed culture here in America, in what is now Mexico and northern South America."

The One Dollar Bill is a Contract!!

"The Great Seal of The MOORISH Nation"

(Look familiar? On the back of the Dollar Bill.)

On the back of the one dollar bill we notice the government seal of the UNITED STATES with the bald eagle holding the olive branch and the arrows. Question? If the eagle encompassed inside of the circle on the right hand side of the bill is a government seal, then what is the pyramid symbol on the left-hand side encompassed inside of a circle. You got it…It's also a government seal! It is the seal of the original government that was already here in this land! That symbol has been flying here in government for thousands of years before the eagle and shield. The eagle and shield is the "sanctioned" government that was allowed to do business here in the ten by ten square mile of land called Washington D.C. As you will notice the word "ONE" is in the middle of the two seals symbolically meaning the two governments are as one. You will also notice that this is the only bill that has not been changed, all the other bills have been colored or the faces enlarged. The one-dollar bill has never and will never change because it is actually a contract between the two nations. Every contract has to have two signatures and on every dollar bill you will see that there are in fact two signatures!

What was done was that the Colonizers try to hide the true meaning of that Moorish pyramid symbol and tell people that the only government in this land is the government under the seal of the eagle and shield, not the original government under the pyramid (the true Republic guaranteed by the Constitution). We have to understand this history to understand the evolution of law, government and their statues, codes and fines that steal our rights and freedoms. As you can see on the following map of the migration of the tribe of Ishmael that the capitol Morocco was where Cleveland Ohio is currently.

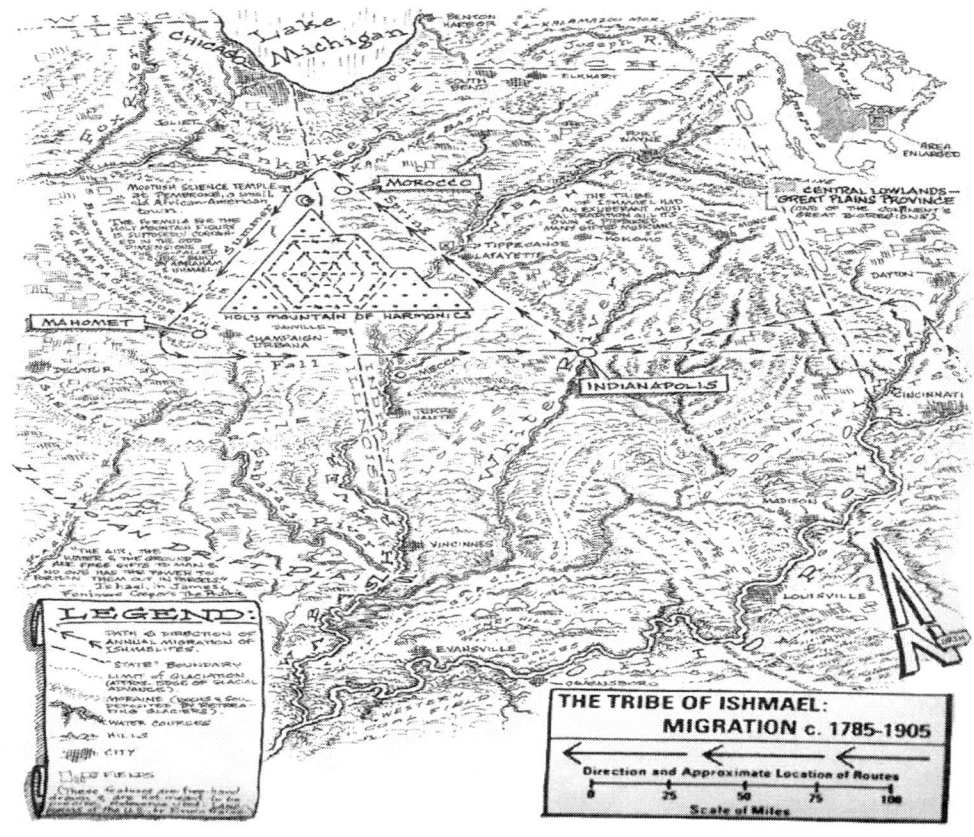

As I previously stated, the Olmec were the first people to inhabit Central America. Guess who are the descendants of the Olmec? **The Mayans**! The Mayans were often referred to as "Black Mexicans" or "Quetzacoat" and are direct descendants of the Malian Moors.

These ancient Mexican wall paintings depict these Moorish Kings as rulers and are unmistakably Moorish. These Moors are responsible for building the pyramids all over South America, Peru, Alaska, Canada and Georgia. Also, All along the Mississippi river and its basins are large mounds of tons of earth built by people who were called the "Mound Builders." The mound builders are descendants of the Malian Moors and the Olmecs.

These Moors eventually migrated to North America from Mexico and became known as the Washataw, the Yamasee, and the Ben Isma-EL tribe. The Ben Isma-El tribe is a collection of the Lenape, Wampanoag and the Natichock Indians who migrated to Illinois, Indiana and Kentucky and referred to themselves as Moors (You can see their migration in the map above with the capitol city MOROCCO). Even then, the Government continued to classify them as Negro in order to strip them of their **_Indigenous rights._**

The Moroccan Treaty of Peace of Friendship of 1787 between the Moorish Nation and The United States Government is the longest standing treaty to date. On the first page of the treaty, you will see that **Thomas Jefferson, John Adams** and **Benjamin Franklin** worked CLOSELY with Moors in the Continental Congress to make sure the treaty was secure. Article six of the Constitution states, "*All debts contracted and <u>engagements entered into</u> **<u>before</u>** the **<u>adoption</u>** of this Constitution, shall be as valid against the United States under this Constitution, as under the Confederation. This Constitution, and the Laws of the United*

States which shall be made in Pursuance thereof; and **all Treaties made, or which shall be made**, *under the Authority of the United States, shall be the supreme Law of the Land;* **and the Judges in every State shall be bound thereby**, *any Thing in the Constitution or Laws of any State to the Contrary notwithstanding."*

Morocco

PEACE AND FRIENDSHIP

Treaty sealed by the Emperor of Morocco June 23, 1786, and delivered to the American agent at Morocco June 28, 1786; additional article signed and sealed on behalf of Morocco July 15, 1786; ship-signals agreement signed at Morocco July 6, 1786.

Entered into force July 15, 1786

Treaty and additional article ratified and proclaimed by the President of the United States July 18, 1787

Expired; replaced January 28, 1837, by treaty of September 16, 1836.

8 Stat. 100; Treaty Series 244-1

TREATY
[TRANSLATION]

To all Persons to whom these Presents shall come or be made known— Whereas the United States of America in Congress assembled by their Commission, bearing date the twelfth day of May One thousand Seven hundred and Eighty four thought proper to constitute John Adams, Benjamin Franklin and Thomas Jefferson their Ministers Plenipotentiary, giving to them or a Majority of them full Powers to confer, treat & negotiate with the Ambassador, Minister or Commissioner of His Majesty the Emperor of Morocco concerning a Treaty of Amity and Commerce, to make & receive propositions for such Treaty and to conclude and sign the same, transmitting it to the United States in Congress assembled for their final Ratification, And by one other Commission bearing date the Eleventh day of March One thousand Seven hundred & Eighty five did further empower the said Ministers Plenipotentiary or a majority of them, by writing under their hands and Seals to appoint such Agent in the said Business as they might think proper with Authority under the directions and Instructions of the said Ministers to commence & prosecute the said Negociations & Conferences for the said Treaty provided that the said Treaty should be signed by the said Ministers: And Whereas, We the said John Adams & Thomas Jefferson two of the said Ministers Plenipotentiary (the said Benjamin Franklin being absent) by writing under the Hand and Seal of the said John Adams at London October the fifth, One thousand Seven hundred and Eighty five, & of the said Thomas Jefferson at Paris October the Eleventh of the same Year, did appoint Thomas Barclay, Agent in the Business aforesaid, giving him the Powers therein, which by the said second Commission we were authorized to give, and the said Thomas Barclay in pursuance thereof, hath arranged Articles for a Treaty of Amity and Commerce between the United States of America and His Majesty the Emperor of Morocco, which Articles written in the Arabic Language, confirmed by His said Majesty the Emperor of Morocco & seal'd with His Royal Seal, being translated into the Language of the said United States of America, together with the Attestations thereto annexed are in the following Words, To Wit.

In the name of Almighty God,

This is a Treaty of Peace and Friendship established between us and the United States of America, which is confirmed, and which we have ordered to be written in this Book and sealed with our Royal Seal at our Court of Morocco on the twenty fifth day of the blessed Month of Shaban, in the Year One thousand two hundred, trusting in God it will remain permanent.

1.

We declare that both Parties have agreed that this Treaty consisting of twenty five Articles shall be inserted in this Book and delivered to the Honorable Thomas Barclay, the Agent of the United States now at our Court, with whose Approbation it has been made and who is duly authorized on their Part, to treat with us concerning all the Matters contained therein.

2.

If either of the Parties shall be at War with any Nation whatever, the other Party shall not take a Commission from the Enemy nor fight under their Colors.

3.

If either of the Parties shall be at War with any Nation whatever and take a Prize belonging to that Nation, and there shall be found on board Subjects or Effects belonging to either of the Parties, the Subjects shall be set at Liberty and the Effects returned to the Owners. And if any Goods belonging to any

114

Thomas Jefferson, John Adams and Benjamin Franklin worked closely with, respected and acknowledged the Moorish Nation as far back as 1787. **_Why is this information not known today by the mass public?_**

TREATY WITH MOROCCO. 1787.   105

Now, KNOW YE, That we, the said John Adams and Thomas Jefferson, Ministers Plenipotentiary aforesaid, do approve and conclude the said treaty, and every article and clause therein contained, reserving the same nevertheless to the United States in Congress assembled, for their final ratification.

In testimony whereof, we have signed the same with our names and seals, at the places of our respective residence, and at the dates expressed under our signatures respectively.

JOHN ADAMS,   (L. S.)
London, January 25th, 1787.

THOMAS JEFFERSON,   (L. S.)
Paris, January 1st, 1787

VOL. VIII.   14

The treaty says "Thus an act was passed in Massachusetts on the 6th of March, 1788, **forbidding any Negro NOT a subject of the Emperor of Morocco**, or a citizen of the United States **from tarrying in the Commonwealth**." Meaning, that those who considered themselves Negro and not Moorish (recognizing their Nationality), could not "Tarry in the

Commonwealth." <u>Those who REMEMBERED that they were Moors used the Moroccan Treaty to **secure their status**</u>. <u>Those who were brainwashed into thinking they were Negros, Descendants of Africans brought by Europeans WERE NOT protected by the Moroccan Treaty, Articles of Confederation or the Constitution.</u>

Another quote from the treaty says, "A petition was presented to the house from sundry free Moors (1790), subjects of the Emperor of Morocco, and residents of the state, praying that **in case they should commit any fault amenable to be brought to justice, that they as subjects to a prince (here in North America) in alliance with the United States of America (via the Treaty of peace and Friendship of 1787), may be tried under the SAME laws as the citizens of the state would be liable to be tried, and NOT under the Negro Act**, which was received and read."

As you can see, you have Moors back in 1787 saying the same thing we are saying now...*THE NATIONALITY OF THE PEOPLE OF COLOR HERE IN THE WESTERN HEMISPHERE IS MOORISH, NOT BLACK, NOT COLORED, NOT ANYTHING ELSE!!*

Do not be mistaken, African-American is not a Nationality, it's a BRAND. Black is not a Nationality it's a BRAND. Puerto-Rican (rich port) is not a Nationality, it's a BRAND. How the name Puerto Rican (Moors mixed with European and Asian) came to be is when translated into English it means "Rich Port." In order to show the families wealth, the women in the family would wear gold around their neck and wrist with no seam to take it off and when the Europeans came and conquered they cut the head and hands off of the women to get the gold...that's why they called it "Rich Port"... it's just a BRAND. Colored is not a Nationality, it's just a BRAND!!! Negro is not a Nationality, it's just a BRAND...Know the difference! Know your true history! ITS ALL ABOUT DIVIDE AND CONQUOR!!!!!!

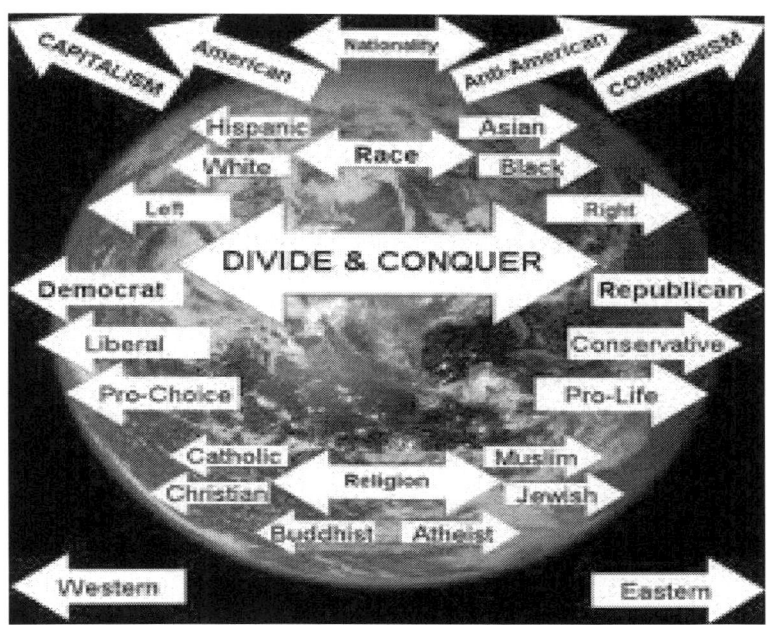

About Letter from <u>George Washington</u>

To the Sultan of Morocco 1789

The letter to the Sultan of Morocco, from President George Washington is one of the favorites amongst the Documents of American History, as it clearly indicates the newly formed "United States of America", under the first Masonic President, George Washington, **was subordinate to and dwelling on the dominions of the**

Moroccan Empire. Anything other than that holds no standing as to why George Washington would write a letter as such to the Sultan of Morocco. It indicates without contradiction that the Moors were in the superior position, that George Washington was the newly appointed President of the United States of America in the North American Continent, under the rule and Dominion of the Sultan of Morocco.

Letter from George Washington to Muhammed Ibn Abdullah - Sultan of Morocco
City of New York December 1, 1789

"Great and Magnanimous Friend,

Since the date of the letter which the late Congress, by their President, addressed to your Imperial Majesty, The United States of America have thought proper to change their government and institute a new one, agreeable to the Constitution, of which I have the honor, herewith, to enclose a copy. The time necessarily employed in the arduous task, and the disarrangements occasioned by so great though peaceable a revolution, will apologize, and account for your Majesty's not having received those regularly advised marks of attention (MONEY) from the United States which the friendship and magnanimity of your conduct toward them afforded reason to expect. The United States, having unanimously appointed me to supreme executive authority in this Nation. Your Majesty's letter of August 17, 1788, which by reason of the dissolution of the late-government, remained unanswered, has been delivered to me. I have also received the letters which Your Imperial Majesty has been so kind as to write, in favor of the United States, to the Bashaws of Tunis and Tripoli, and I present to you the sincere acknowledgements and thanks of the United States for this important mark of your friendship for them. We greatly regret the hostile disposition of those regencies toward this nation, who have never injured them, is not to be removed, on terms of our power to comply with. Within our territories (WASHINGTON DC) there are no mines, wither of gold or silver, and this young nation just recovering from the waste and dissolution of a long war, have not, as yet, had time to acquire riches by agriculture and commerce. But our soil is bountiful, and our people industrious, and we have reason to flatter ourselves that we shall gradually become useful to our friends.

The encouragement which **Your Majesty** has been pleased, generously, to give to our commerce **<u>with your dominions</u>** (meaning your lands), the punctuality with which you have caused the **Treaty with us** (Treaty of Peace and Friendship 1787) to be observed, and the just and generous measures taken in the case of Captain Proctor, make a deep impression on the United States and confirm their respect for and attachment to Your Imperial Majesty. It gives me great pleasure to have the opportunity of assuring Your Majesty that, while I remain at the head of this nation, I shall not cease to promote every measure that may conduce to the friendship and harmony which so happily subsist between your Empire and them, and shall esteem myself happy in every occasion of convincing Your Majesty of the high sense (which in common with the whole nation) I entertain the magnanimity, wisdom and benevolence of Your Majesty. May the Almighty bless Your Imperial Majesty, our Great and Magnanimous friend, with His constant guidance and protection.

- George Washington"

Actual HAND-WRITTEN letter below:

> **Moor** (mūəɹ, mōəɹ), *sb.*² Forms: 4 **Maur**, 4–7 **More**, 5 **Moure**, **Mowre**, 6, 8 **Maure**, 6–7 **Moore**, 7– **Moor**. (Now with initial capital.) [ME. *More*, a. F. *More* (13th c.), *Maure*, ad. L. *Maurus* (med. L. *Mōrus*), Gr. Μαῦρος. Cf. Sp., Pg., It. *Moro*; MDu. *Moor*, *Moer* (Du. *Moor*), OHG. *Môr*, pl. *Môri* (MHG. *Môr*, *Mœr*, mod.G. *Mohr*).
> The L. *Maurus*, Gr. Μαῦρος may possibly be from some ancient North African language. Some believe the word to be merely a use of Gr. μαῦρος black (which on this view is aphetic from ἀμαυρός blind); but this adj. (or at least this sense of it) is confined to late Gr., and may even be derived from the ethnic name.]
>
> **1.** In *Ancient History*, a native of *Mauretania*, a region of Northern Africa corresponding to parts of Morocco and Algeria. In later times, one belonging to the people of mixed Berber and Arab race, Mohammedan in religion, who constitute the bulk of the population of North-western Africa, and who in the 8th c. conquered Spain. In the Middle Ages, and as late as the 17th c., the Moors were commonly supposed to be mostly black or very swarthy (though the existence of 'white Moors' was recognized), and hence the word was often used for 'negro'; cf. BLACKAMOOR.

<u>As you see above, the term MOOR was used to describe our people as early as the 8th Century and as late as the 17th Century!</u>

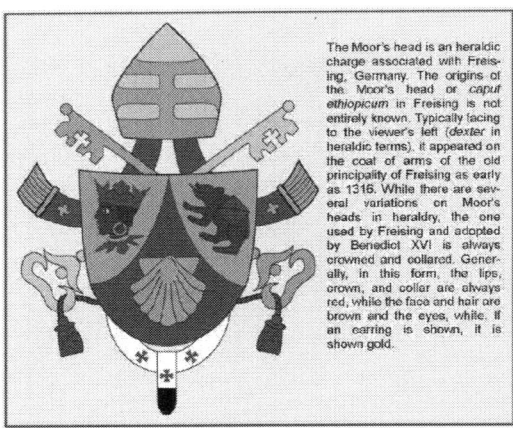

Here sits "The Pope", who came to New York -- the Empire State, and sat under the Moors Head, while those who are descendants of Moors, debate as to the impacting validity of the honor of THEIR direct ancestors.

The coat of arms of Benedict XVI in the garden behind Saint Peter's Basilica.

The Coat of arms of Pope Benefict XVI as seen on the tapestry hanging from Saint Peter's Basilica in Rome. The embroidered arms were display for the Palm Sunday services in 2006. This photograph was taken by Eva on 9 April 2006.

Below are 18 Of the Moorish Nobility Moorish Family Crest in Germany. These Moorish Nobility Family Crest Were Uncovered by Joel Rogers, who was a Nuwbun Historian Born In Jamaica. It Has Been Said That Jo-El Rogers Found More Than 500 Images of Moorish Noble Families In Europe, Much Like The Ones Below. Just Imagine 500 Moorish Nobility Families Crest That Are Purposely Being Hidden from The Public To Conceal The Truth. This Leaves Another Tremendous Problem for Them, Because This Is In Europe, Not Africa!

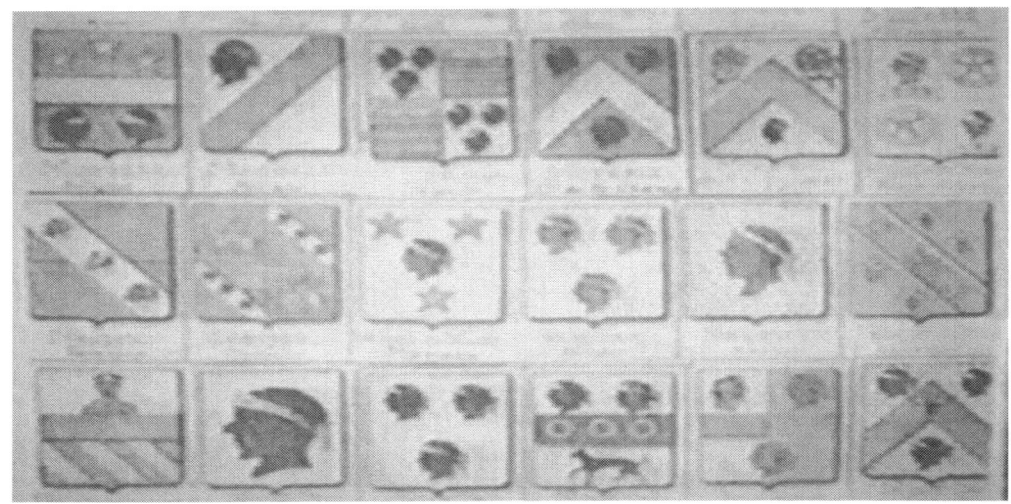

"These are Moorish Nobles Coat of Arms, which are registered in Europe as royal families, NOT slaves and cotton pickers."

The Iroquois (Moorish) Confederacy

The structure of the Iroquois Confederacy inspired the American Colonists' development of the U.S. government. On June 11, 1776 while the question of independence was being debated, the visiting Iroquois chiefs were formally invited into the meeting hall of the Continental Congress. There a speech was delivered, in which they were addressed as "Brothers" and told of the delegates' wish that the "friendship" between them would "continue as long as the sun shall shine" and the "waters run." The speech also expressed the hope that the new Americans and the Iroquois act "as one people, and have but one heart." After this speech, an Onondaga chief requested permission to give Hancock an

Indian name. The Congress graciously consented, and so the president was renamed "Karanduawn, or the Great Tree." With the Iroquois chiefs inside the halls of Congress on the eve of American Independence, **the impact of Iroquois ideas on the founders is unmistakable.** History is indebted to Charles Thomson, an adopted European into the Delaware Moors, whose knowledge of and respect for American Indians (Moors) is reflected in the attention that he gave to this ceremony in the records of the Continental Congress.

"(The Iroquois League) was a model social order in many ways superior to the white man's culture of the day and its form of government more nearly approached perfection than any that has been tried to date." -- Elmore Reaman 1967

Because historians tend to focus on military engagements and changes in national boundaries, our population has little understanding of cultural and social interactions. In an interesting twist of interpretation, Felix Cohen proposed, in a 1952 article called "Americanizing the White Man," That "(historians) have seen America only as an imitation of Europe," but that "the real epic of America is the yet unfinished story of the Americanization of the white man."

He defines Americanism as largely a product of the influence of Indian (Moorish) culture on the white European settlers. In an equally bold statement, Francis Jennings in The Invasion of America: Indians, Colonialism and The Cant of Conquest (1975) states that "What white (American) society owes to Indian society, as much as to any other source, is the mere fact of its existence."

Early Euro-Americans voluntarily adopted methods, lifestyles, artifacts, and ideas from the indigenous people, often in order to survive. Moors in America provided half the modern world's domesticated food crops, numerous herbal medicines, clothing, transportation pathways and modes, crafts and artifacts, hygiene methods, and thousands of words including place names and ideas of governance that blended ideals of rugged individuality with concern for the common welfare.

The Iroquois republic had continuously existed since the 14th or 15th century. In 1930, Arthur Pound 's Johnson of the Mohawk states, wrote "with the possible exception of the also unwritten British Constitution, deriving from the Magna Carta, the Iroquois Constitution is the longest-existing international constitution in the world." Known as "The Great Law of Peace," this orally transmitted constitution describes a federal union of five (later six) Indian nations: Mohawk, Onondagam Seneca, Oneida, Cayuga and the Tscarora, adopted in 1715. It was only put in writing in 1915 by Arthur C. Parker, archeologist for the State Museum of New York.

The Europeans and Iroquois of the mid-18th century were on more friendly terms. Many English nobles adopted the lifestyle of Indians and joined their nations. The Treaty Councils brought cultural exchanges in which leaders and statesmen met as equals to diplomatically solve problems and alleviate strained relations. The trade of Great Britain and the peace and prosperity of the colonies was dependent upon this alliance.

During the era, Benjamin Franklin published twenty-six treaty accounts and represented the state of Pennsylvania as an Indian (Moorish) commissioner. In the pre-Revolutionary period, when he and his friends were advocating a federal union of the colonies, no European model was found to be suitable. That's why there were three different constitutions before our present Constitution today (Declaration of Independence, the Bill of Rights, Articles of Confederation, then the present Constitution). Franklin's contact with the Iroquois influenced many key ideas for a new form of government (federalism, equality, natural rights, freedom of religion, property rights, etc). At the 1744 treaty council, by Franklin's account, Canassatego, speaker for the great council at Onondaga, recommended that the colonies form a union in common defense under a federal government: "We are a powerful Confederacy, and by your observing the same methods our wise forefathers have taken, you will acquire much strength and power; therefore, whatever befalls you, do not fall out with one another."

In arguing for such a plan, Franklin stressed the fact that the individual nations of the confederacy managed their own internal affairs without interference from the Grand Council.

Twenty years after Franklin's plan was defeated at the Albany congress, it reappeared in the Declaration of Independence and the Articles of Confederation. Franklin, Jefferson, John Adams, and George Washington were all familiar with the Iroquois polity. The integration of this knowledge into their theories of utopias and natural societies further inspired the U.S. founding fathers.

Each of the Iroquois nations was represented to the Confederate Council by a lord of the confederacy and one war chief. Their league included a system of checks and balances, and no action could be taken without the approval of all five Indian nations. Their notions of equality and liberty extended to women as well as men. In war, they never enslaved captives but offered to adopt those willing to accept the Great Law. Their own members could be alienated or expelled by not following the Great Law, and a non-member could be adopted by proposal or invitation with approval from the lords.

In their constitution, the lords of the confederacy are described as mentors and spiritual guides of the people; their hearts are to be full of peace and goodwill, and their minds full of yearning for the welfare of the people, including those of future generations, their words and actions are to be marked by calm deliberation. They must be honest and have no self-interest; if they become wayward they receive warnings first from the clan women then from the men. If they persist in negative behaviors, they ultimately lose their position and possibly their life. The lords are poorer than the common people. They own few material possessions, and give away presents or plunder acquired by treaty or war. They are above pettiness and corruption, and show no signs of selfishness.

Those who recognized the wisdom and long history of the Iroquois government did not consider the Indians as mere "savages." Like the Iroquois, Thomas Jefferson believed that public opinion and popular consent were key in maintaining freedom and good government. He held that the power of public opinion was an important reason for the Iroquois' lack of oppressive government and class differences, and for the power to impeach officials who offended governing principles. Like the Iroquois, he also believed that the best government is the least government.

In oratory, the Europeans compared the Iroquois with the Greeks and Romans. Both emphasized ethical proof in their arguments. The Indians (Moors) ended their orations with the words *hiro* and *kone*. *Hiro* means "I have said," and *kone* was spoken as an exclamation of joy or sorrow, depending on the occasion and circumstances. **The French pronunciation of these words together became "Iroquois."**

Unlike Europe, the Iroquois society was matri-lineal. Women owned the land and the status of their lineage. They owned all possessions of their husbands after marriage except their horse and rifle; they took charge off the money, and were the tribe's educators and communicators of tradition. They female heirs of the lords of the confederacy were called royaneh (noble). The lord of the confederacy was nominated by women and selected for qualities of trustworthiness, good character, honesty, faithfulness to the people and the nation, support of the family, and good management of personal affairs. There was not state religion, and the religious rites and festivals of each nation were safeguarded against being disturbed or interrupted. Civil duties were separated from those of the religious leaders, and festivals were held in the longhouses.

In examining the vision of our forefathers and the many hundreds of years of the Iroquois confederacy's success, we see how far we have strayed in just over two hundred years. More and more a nation of law and order, with vast class and economic distinctions and political favoritism, we would do well to reeducate ourselves in the values of the Iroquois (Moors) honesty, good character, honor, the power of the spoken word and public opinion, and the high status of women.

Documents YOU MUST know!!!

1. FREE MOORISH-AMERICAN ZODIAC CONSTITUTION: (Zodiac Constitution and Birthrights of the Moorish Americans) being Ali, Bey, El, Dey and Al), Article two (2), Paragraph two (2).

2. UNITED STATES REPUBLIC: DEPARTMENT OF JUSTICE: Moorish American Credentials: AA 222141- TRUTH A-1

3. UNITED STATES SUPREME COURT: SUPREME LAW – Acts of State

4. UNITED STATES REPUBLIC CONSTITUTION: Article III (3), Section two (2), Amendment V (5) (Liberty clause) and Amendment IX (9) (Reservation of the Rights of the People).

5. RESOLUTION NUMBER SEVENTY-FIVE (75): Dated April 17, 1933 A.D. (MOORISH-AMERICAN SOCIETY OF PHILADELPHIA AND THE USE OF THEIR NAMES),

6. UNIVERSAL DECLARATION OF HUMAN RIGHTS – UNITED NATIONS – HUMAN RIGHTS [Article Fifteen (15)].

7. RIGHTS OF INDIGENOUS PEOPLES – UNITED NATIONS: GENERAL ASSEMBLY – Part 1, Article 4.

8. Treaty of Peace and Friendship of 1787

9. The Declaration of the Granting of Independence to Colonial Countries and People UN GA #1514

10. The American Declaration of the Rights and Duties of Man' (Adopted by the Ninth International Conference of American States Bogota, Colombia, 1948 at Article 5, Article 17, Article 26

11. Declaration on the Principles of International Law

12. Executive Order Number: 13107, 63, Federal Register, 68,991 (1998)- Implementation of Human Rights Treaties

13. The Moors Sundry Act of 1790

Lesson #3

The Truth about: Commerce

Employers take with-holdings, referred to as "income taxes" from your payroll check. It is important for you to know that your Salary, or labor compensation is **NOT INCOME. Income is PROFITS from a Capitol investment**. Many agree that their labor compensation or Salary is Income by signing W-2's and W-4's. Thus, they contract through the With-Holding Agent (employer), with the IRS (a private corporation).

You are contracting with the IRS, via your Employer, and giving them the authority to continue taking finances from you. To pay, or not pay these taxes is voluntary, therefore it is YOUR decision. When you violate the contract, you made by not terminating it properly, the IRS threatens to take you to TAX COURT, of which there is no such thing as Tax Court. It is usually an administrative hearing, held in some room or office. Thus, in actuality they are taking you to "court" for breach of contract

When most people think of the IRS (Internal Revenue Service) they get a sick feeling in their stomach especially around April 15th of each year. What most people do not understand is that the IRS has committed Fraud on the American people.

Now after reading this do not go run out and stop paying your income taxes or that NMC Services told you to stop paying your income taxes. We are just sharing with you the truth, if you decide to stop paying income taxes you must study and choose your battles wisely for the IRS can be brutal, they can take your house, use guns and even take you to jail if you do not know what you are doing.

For us to fully understand the IRS Fraud we have to travel back in time to when a group of international bankers got together and congress created the 1871 Act.

To fully understand you have to understand what the 1871 Act is and who created it. Act of 1871 which established in the District of Columbia, we have been living under the UNITED STATES CORPORATION which is owned by certain international bankers and aristocracy of Europe and Britain.

In 1871 the Congress changed the name of the original Constitution by changing ONE WORD -- and that was very significant as you will read.

Some people do not understand that ONE WORD or TWO WORDS difference in any "legal" document DO make the critical difference. But, Congress has known, and does know, this.

February 21, 1871 Congress Passes an Act to Provide a Government for the District of Columbia, also known as the Act of 1871. With no constitutional authority to do so, Congress creates a separate form of government for the District of Columbia, a ten mile square parcel of land (see, Acts of the Forty-first Congress," Section 34, Session III, chapters 61 and 62).

The act -- passed when the country was weakened and financially depleted in the aftermath of the Civil War -- was a strategic move by foreign interests (international bankers) who were intent upon gaining a stranglehold on the coffers and neck of America.

Congress cut a deal with the international bankers (specifically Rothschilds of London) to incur a DEBT to said bankers. Because the bankers were not about to lend money to a floundering nation without serious stipulations, they devised a way to get their foot in the door of the United States.

The Act of 1871 formed a corporation called THE UNITED STATES. The corporation, OWNED by foreign interests, moved in and shoved the original Constitution into a dustbin.

The IRS (Internal Revenue Service) is its own Incorporation and conflict to popular belief is not even part of the US Government Incorporation, they just let you believe that it is.

Filing a federal income tax return is, **in fact, voluntary,** because there is no statute or regulation that requires the vast majority of U.S. citizens to file and pay income taxes or to have taxes withheld from the money they earn. Neither the IRS nor the Congress can cite an authorizing law or regulation. Is that IRS Fraud or what?

Joseph R. (Joe) Banister is a former IRS Criminal Investigation Division Special Agent who learned of serious constitutional questions relating to the federal income tax and the federal banking and monetary systems. Mr. Banister's expertise in the fields of accounting, finance, taxation, and law enforcement enabled him to not only understand these issues but realize that he could play a role in bringing the issues fraud into the public arena for analysis and debate.

Citizens cannot "voluntarily" file a federal income tax return without surrendering their 5th amendment right not to bear witness against themselves. You can be criminally prosecuted for your "voluntary" return.

The IRS Incorporation was created in Costa Rica to collect trade tariffs and taxes for products going in and out of Latin American countries. Their office resides in Washington D.C which is purchased land by a native of this country but then given to the US Government it does not belong to the people of the United States for America, just like Alaska and Hawaii do not belong to the people but is purchased land given to the US Government Incorporation.

Marcey Brooks one of the stars in American Freedom to Fascism as a juror on the

Whitey Harrell IRS tax case that made a stand to the judge, "**show us were the law is that this man is required to pay income taxes to the IRS and we will find him guilty**", no law was ever given to the jury and the jury found Whitey Harrell <u>**NOT GUILTY**</u>!!!

The Wizard of OZ – an allegory...

An allegory (parable) is the expression of truths about human conduct and experience by means of symbolic fictional figures and actions. No movie does that better than "The Wizard of Oz", an allegory of the state of affairs we now live in today, an allegory of the unfolding deception that was instituted in America via the stock-market crash of 1929 and the bankruptcy of the United States in 1933. The setting of this allegory is in Kansas, the "heartland" of America (Coincidentally the geographical **center** of the U.S.A).

In came the twister, the whirling confusion of the **Great Depression, the stock-market crash, the U.S. Bankruptcy, and the theft of America's gold**. When Dorthy was whisked away, her world was black and white and once she landed, the world was "colored". In law, when something is "colored" it is not real or not true (ARTIFICIAL). In order for Dorthy to find the Wizard, she had to "follow the yellow-brick road" (the gold-bar road). Even the title "The Wizard of OZ" says a lot because gold in measured in ounces (Oz). This gold reference is reference to the UNITED STATES not having any gold to back the currency after 1933. The saying in the movie was we have to "follow the yellow brick road (gold road)" to get back "home" or back to what's real and not artificial.

"STRAWMAN"

Coincidentally, the first person that Dorthy ran into was the STRAWMAN. As we have been shown, the STRAWMAN is your "transmitting utility", the way your natural person navigates through in the fictitious world. The STRAWMAN is the first person that Dorthy meets because he is the one who she needs to navigate the fictitious Land of Oz.

"T.I.N. Man"

Dorthy continued to walk down the yellow brick road (Gold), when Dorthy came across the tin-man. The tin-man had an ax in his hand and was frozen midway through a chop. This is symbolic of the working man or woman. The tin-man is a symbol for our Taxpayer-Identification-Number. The (TIN) man, is a hollow man of tin, a vessel, or vehicle used for tracking employees. Your Tax Identification Number is your nine-digit SOCIAL SECURITY NUMBER, and you have used it for every commercial transition that your STRAWMAN has done.

"Cowardly Lion"

The cowardly lion represented the "brown colored" original people of the land. These people were people who were once kings but lost their identity and their culture and became "cowardly lions". This was a symbol of the indigenous people who did not know their rightful status, birthright and royal bloodline in the land.

Wicked Witch of the West

The tactic of the Wicked Witch of the West was to drug them into unconsciousness by covering the countryside with poppy flowers, poppies (the source of heroin, opium, and morphine) and then waltz in and snatch the slippers. In other words, the best way to loot the gold was to dull the senses of the American people with a contrived crisis (Drugs, the Great Depression). And of course, now we have illicit street drugs, heroin, cocaine, etc., and legal drugs such as Ridlin, etc. and television, bogus media dishing out control propaganda,

The poppy-drugs worked on Dorothy, the lion and Toto (the flesh-and-blood entities) but had no effect on the scarecrow or the tin-man (the artificial entities). The two cried out for help, and Glenda (the Good Witch of the North) answered their cries with a blanket of snow that nullified the narcotic effect of the poppies on Dorothy, Toto, and the lion.

As they all scampered toward the Emerald City, the city of green, (Federal Reserve Notes...the new fiat money - money by decree) we hear the Munchkins singing the glories of the Wizard's Creation (The fiat green Federal Reserve Notes).

Your Birth Certificate is worth $$$$$

When a child is born, the hospital generally sends the original, not a copy, of this record of live birth to the State Bureau of Vital Statistics, sometimes called the Department of Health and Rehabilitative Services (HRS). Each STATE is required to supply the corporate UNITED STATES with birth, death, and health statistics. The STATE agency that receives the original record of live birth keeps it and then issues another Birth Certificate in a different form where the name of the baby is spelled in ALL CAPITAL LETTERS. This creates a 'legal person' as opposed to a natural individual.

The Birth Certificate issued by the State is then registered with the U.S. Department of Commerce - - the Executive Office - specifically through their own sub-agency, the U.S. Census Bureau, which is responsible to register vital statistics from all the states. Thus, the birth certificate is registered in international commerce. The word registered, as it is used in commercial law, does not mean that the ALL CAPITAL version of the name was "merely" noted or recorded in a book for future reference purposes. When a birth certificate is registered with the U.S. Department of Commerce, the Treasury will issue a <u>bond</u> on the value of the birth certification. That bond is then made available for purchase on a securities exchange and is bought by the Federal Reserve <u>Bank</u>. This purchase then become the authority or collateral to issue <u>Federal Reserve</u> Notes, which we use as a medium of exchange.

The value of the bond in today's world around $650,000-1,000,000. The bond is then held in trust for the Federal Reserve at the Depository Trust Corporation at 55 Water Street in New York City, about two blocks down the street from the Federal Reserve. It is a high-rise office building and the sign in front reads: "The Tower of Power."

This process creates a burden in that the ALL-CAPITAL legal person named on the birth certificate has become a surety, or guarantor, a condition and obligation that is automatically and unwittingly assumed unless you rebut the presumption by effectively noticing government.

"Guarantor. Person who becomes secondarily liable for another's debt or performance... One who promises to answer for the debt, default or miscarriage of another." - Black's Law Dictionary, Sixth Edition

From this it is easy to conclude that the baby is to assume the liability for any burden created or associated with the strawman or <u>trade</u> name listed on the birth certificate. It is not difficult to see that a state - created birth certificate with an ALL-CAPS name is a document, evidencing debt the moment it is issued. Once a state has registered a birth document with U.S. Department of Commerce, the Department notifies the Treasury Department, which takes out a loan from the Federal Reserve. The Treasury uses the <u>loan</u> to purchase a bond (the Fed holds a "purchase <u>money</u> security interest" in the bond) from the Department of Commerce, which invests the sale proceeds in the stock or bond market.

The child just became the slave ... can you see how this has happened? Until you take control, in other words "rebut", you will remain the slave. Slaves do not have freedoms.... and that is what we all (or almost all have been since the day we were born, and our innocent parents, and their parents, and their parents.... before us. Every citizen is given a BOND number (the red number on the Birth Certificate) and each live birth is valued at from 650,000 to 750,000 Federal Reserve dollars in collateral from the Fed.

Let's take a look at the Birth Certificate [**below**]. You will see the red numbers and you will see the fact that it is, in reality, a "Bank Note." Congratulations, you and I are commodities!

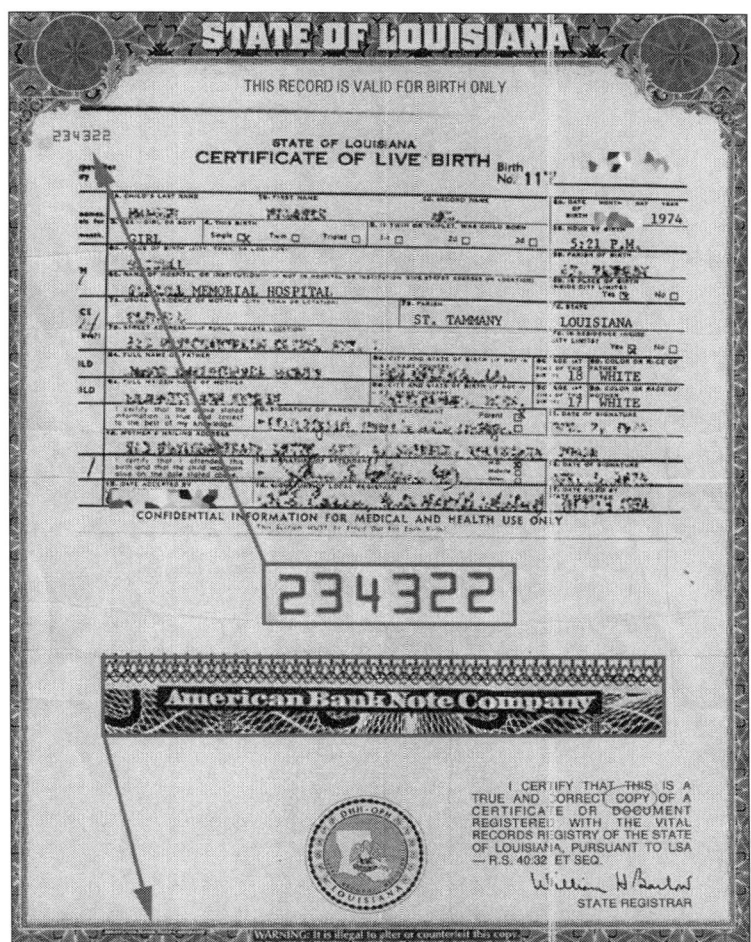

Names in "ALL CAPS" on Birth Certificates

Since the early 1960s, State governments have issued Birth Certificates to "persons" with legal fictional names using "ALL CAPS" names. This is not a lawful record of your physical birth, but rather the acknowledgement of the "birth" of the juristic, all-caps name. It may appear to be your true name, but since no proper name is ever written in all caps (either lawfully or grammatically) it does not identify who you are. The Birth Certificate is the government's self-created document of title for its new property, you and me! In a way, it makes us a kind of corporation whose company name is the same as our real name, but written in ALL CAPS. This "corporation" then generates taxes and wealth over its lifetime and in this way, repays the collateral that Uncle Sam borrowed from the Federal Reserve.

Remember that "Bond" thing printed on the bottom of the certificate?

Bond: A usually formal written agreement by which a person undertakes to perform a certain act (as fulfill the obligations of a contract) . . with the condition that failure to perform or abstain will obligate the person. . to pay a sum of money or will result in the forfeiture of money put up by the person or surety. 1: One who acts as a surety. 2: An interest-bearing document giving evidence of a debt issued by a government body or corporation that is sometimes secured by a lien on property and is often designed to take care of a particular financial need. -- Ibid. -- Merriam-Webster Dictionary of Law (1996).

Banknote: A kind of negotiable instrument, a promissory note made by a bank payable to the bearer on demand, used as money, and in many jurisdictions, is legal tender. Along with coins, banknotes make up the cash or bearer forms of all modern money.

Birth certificates are a form of securities called "warehouse receipts." The items included on a warehouse receipt, as descried at Â§7-202 of the Uniform Commercial Code, the law which governs commercial paper and transactions, which parallel a birth certificate are:

- the location of the warehouse where the goods are stored...(residence)
- the date of issue of the receipt.....("Date issued")
- the consecutive number of the receipt...(found on back or front of the certificate, usually in red numbers)
- a description of the goods or of the packages containing them...(name, sex, date of birth, etc.)
- the signature of the warehouseman, which may be made by his authorized agent... (municipal clerk or state registrar's signature)

Birth certificates now appear to at least qualify as "warehouse receipts" under the Uniform Commercial Code. Black's Law Dictionary, 7th ed. defines:

Warehouse Receipt. "...A warehouse receipt, which is considered a document of title, may be a negotiable instrument and is often used for financing with inventory as security." It is not difficult to see that a state-created Birth Certificate, with an ALL CAPS name is a document evidencing debt the moment it is issued.

Once a state has registered a birth document with the U.S. Department of Commerce, the Department notifies the Treasury Department, which takes out a loan from the Federal Reserve. The Treasury uses the loan to purchase a bond (the Fed holds a purchase money security interest in the bond) from the Department of Commerce, which invests the sale proceeds in the stock or bond market. The Treasury Department then issues Treasury securities in the form of Treasury Bonds, Notes, and Bills using the bonds as surety for the new securities.

This cycle is based on the future tax revenues of the legal person whose name appears on the Birth Certificate. This also means that the bankrupt, <u>corporate</u> U.S. can guarantee to the purchasers of their securities the lifetime labor and tax revenues of every citizen of the United States/American with a Birth Certificate as collateral for payment. This device is initiated simply by converting the lawful, true name of the child into a legal, juristic name of a person.

Legally, you are considered to be a slave or indentured servant to the various Federal, State and local governments via your STATE-issued and STATE-created Birth Certificate in the name of your all-caps person. Birth Certificates are issued so that the issuer can claim *exclusive* title to the legal person created thereby.

How can this Birth Certificate Bond be Used to Our Advantage?

You Can Discharge Almost Any Debt with Proper Use of the UCC

You can discharge any debt attached to your STRAWMAN such as Secured Loans, Credit Card Debt, Student Loans, Auto Loans, Assessments, Citations, Debts, Demands, Fines, Penalties, Tax Liens and Judgments. Debt Discharge and "Accepted for Value" is based on understanding how you've been misled, and learning what to do about it!

The History of How We Were Put Into the "Commerce Game"

As you have read, On April 5, 1933, then President Franklin Delano Roosevelt, under Executive Order, issued April 5, 1933, declared: "All persons are required to deliver on or before May 1, 1933 all Gold Coin, Gold Bullion, and Gold Certificates now owned by them to a Federal Reserve Bank, branch or agency, or to any member bank of the Federal Reserve System."

The order (proclamation) issued by Roosevelt was an undisciplined act of treason. Two months after the Executive Order, on June 5, 1933, the Senate and House of Representatives, 73d Congress, 1st session, at 4:30 P.M. approve House Joint Resolution 192 (HJR-192) A Joint Resolution to suspend the Gold Standard and abrogate the Gold Clause, Joint resolution to assure uniform value to the coins and currencies of the United States.

HJR-192 states, in part, that "Every provision contained in or made with respect to any obligation which purports to give the oblige a right to require payment in gold or a particular kind of coin or currency, or in any amount of money of the United States measured thereby, is declared to be against public policy, and no such provision shall be contained in or made with respect to any obligation hereafter incurred. Every obligation, heretofore or hereafter incurred, whether or not any such provisions is contained therein or made with respect thereto, shall be discharged upon payment, dollar for dollar, in any such coin or currency which at the time of payment is legal tender for public and private debts."

HJR-192 goes on to state: "As used in this resolution, the term 'obligation' means an obligation (including every obligation of and to the United States, excepting currency) payable in money of the United States; and the term 'coin or currency' means coin or currency of the United States, including Federal Reserve notes and circulating notes of Federal Reserve banks and national banking associations."

HJR-192 superseded Public Law, replacing it with public policy. **This eliminated our ability to PAY our debts, allowing us only to DISCHARGE then.** When we use any commercial paper (checks, federal reserve notes, etc.), and accept it as money, we simply pass the unpaid debt attached to the paper on to others, by way of our purchases and transactions. This unpaid debt, under public policy, now carries a public liability for its collection. In other words, all debt is now public.

The United States government, in order to provide necessary goods and services, created a commercial bond (birth certificate), by pledging the property, labor, life and body of its citizens, as payment for the debt (bankruptcy). This commercial bond made chattel (property) out of every man, woman and child in the United States. We became nothing more than "human resources" and collateral for the debt. This was without our knowledge and/or our consent.

The United States government officials took (and still do, to this day) certified copies of all our birth certificates and placed them in the United States Department of Commerce as registered securities. These securities, each of which carries an estimated $1,000,000 (one million) dollar value, have been (and still are) circulated around the world as collateral for loans, entries on the asset side of ledgers, etc., just like any other security. There's just one problem, we didn't authorize it.

The United States is a District of Columbia corporation. In Volume 20: Corpus Juris Section 1785 we find "The United States government is a foreign corporation with respect to a State"

(see: NY re: Merriam 36 N.E. 505 1441 S. 0.1973, 14 L. Ed. 287).

Since a corporation is a fictitious "person" (it cannot speak, see, touch, smell, etc.), it cannot, by itself, function in the real world. It needs a conduit, a transmitting utility, a liaison of some sort, to "connect" the fictional person, and fictional world in which it exists, to the real world.

Living people exist in a real world, not a fictional, virtual world. But government does exist in a fictional world, and can only deal directly with other fictional or virtual persons, agencies, states, etc. In order for a fictional person to deal with real people there must be a connection, a liaison, and a go-between. This can be something as simple as a contract. When both "persons," the real and the fictional, agree to the terms of a contract, there is a connection, intercourse, dealings, there is a communication, an exchange. There is business! But there is another way for fictional government to deal with the real man and woman: through the use of a representative, a liaison, and the go-between. Who is this go-between, this liaison that connects fictional government to real men and women? It's a government created shadow, a fictional man or woman ... with the same name as ours.

This PERSON was created by using our birth certificates as the Manufacturer's Certificate of Origin (MCO) and the state in which we were born as the "port of entry". This gave fictional government a fictional PERSON with whom to deal directly. This PERSON is a strawman.

STRAMINEUS HOMO: Latin: A man of straw, one of no substance, put forward as bail or surety. This definition comes from *Black's Law Dictionary, 6th. Edition, page 1421.*

Following the definition of STRAMINEUS HOMO in Black's Law Dictionary, we find the next word, Strawman. STRAWMAN: A front, a third party who is put up in name only to take part in a transaction. Nominal party to a transaction; one who acts as an agent for another for the purposes of taking title to real property and executing whatever documents and instruments the principal may direct. Person who purchases property for another to conceal identity of real purchaser or to accomplish some purpose otherwise not allowed.

Webster's Ninth New Collegiate Dictionary defines the term "strawman" as: 1: a weak or imaginary opposition set up only to be easily confuted 2: a person set up to serve as a cover for a usually questionable transaction.

The Strawman can be summed up as an imaginary, passive stand-in for the real participant; a front; a blind; a person regarded as a nonentity. The Strawman is a "shadow", a go-between. For quite some time a rather large number of people in this country have known that a man or woman's name, written in ALL CAPS, or last name first, does not identify real, living people. Taking this one step further, the rules of grammar for the English language have no provisions for the abbreviation of people's names, i.e. initials are not to be used. As an example, John Adam Smith is correct. ANYTHING else is not correct. Not Smith, John Adam or Smith, John A. or J. Smith or J. A. Smith or JOHN ADAM SMITH or SMITH, JOHN or any other variation. NOTHING, other than John Adam Smith identifies the real, living man. All other appellations identify either a deceased man or a fictitious man: such as a corporation or a STRAWMAN.

Over the years government, through its "public" school system, has managed to pull the wool over our eyes and keep US ignorant of some very important facts. Because all facets of the media (print, radio, television) have an ever-increasing influence in our lives, and because media is controlled (with the issuance of licenses, etc.) by government and its agencies, we have slowly and systematically been led to believe that any form/appellation of our names is, in fact, still us: as long as the spelling is correct. WRONG!

Everything, Since June 1933, Operates in COMMERCE!

Commerce is based on agreement, on contract. Government has an implied agreement with the STRAWMAN (government's creation) and the STRAWMAN is subject to government rule, as we illustrated above. But when we, the real flesh and blood man and woman, step into their "process" we become the "surety" for the fictitious STRAWMAN. Reality and fiction are reversed. We then become liable for the debts, liabilities and obligations of the STRAWMAN, relinquishing our real (protected) character as we stand up for the fictional STRAWMAN.

In order to place the STRAWMAN in the fictional world and ourselves in the real world (with all our "shields" in place against fictional government) we must send a non-negotiable (private) "Charge Back" and a nonnegotiable "Bill of Exchange" to the United States Secretary of Treasury, along with a copy of our birth certificate, the evidence, the MCO, of the STRAWMAN. By doing this we discharge our portion of the public debt, releasing us, the real man or woman, from the debts, liabilities and obligations of the STRAWMAN. Those debts, liabilities and obligations exist in the fictional commercial world of "book entries", on computers and/or in paper ledgers. It is a world of "digits" and "notes", not of money and substance. Property of the real man once again becomes tax exempt and free from levy, as it must be in accord with HJR-192.

Sending the nonnegotiable Charge Back and Bill of Exchange will access our Treasury Direct Account (TDA). What is our Treasury Direct Account? According to one theorist, it is a pledge that was made for each birth certificate in the amount of $630,000 (another pegs it at $1,000,000). Thus everybody and everything in the United States is simply collateral for the bonds issued by the U.S. government.

This $1,000,000 (one million) account is for the STRAWMAN, the fictional "person" with the name in all caps and/or last name first. It is there for the purpose of making book entries, to move figures, "digits" from one side of ledgers to the other. Without constant movement, a shark will die and quite ironically, like the shark, there must also be constant movement in commerce, or it too will die. Figures, digits, the entries in ledgers must move from asset side to debit side and back again, or commerce dies. No movement, no commerce.

The fictional person of government can only function in a fictional commercial world, one where there is no real money, only fictional funds ... mere entries, figures, and digits. A presentment from fictional government (whether traffic citation or criminal charges) is a negative, commercial "claim" against the STRAWMAN. This "claim" takes place in the commercial, fictional world of government. "Digits" move from one side of your STRAWMAN account to the other, or to a different account. This is today's commerce.

Playing the Commerce Game

What if we learned how to control the flow and movement of entries, figures, and digits, for our own benefit? Is that possible? How can the real man in the real world, function in the fictional world in which the commerce game exists?

When in commerce do as commerce does, use the Uniform Commercial Code (UCC). The UCC-1 Financing Statement is the one contract in the world that can NOT be broken and it's the foundation of the Accepted for Value process. The power of this document is awesome.

Since the TDA exists for the STRAWMAN (who, until now, has been controlled by government), we can gain control (and ownership) of the STRAWMAN by first activating the TDA and then filing an UCC-1 Financing Statement. This does two things for us.

First, by activating the TDA we gain limited control over the funds in the account. This allows us to also move entries, figures, and digits **for *our* benefit**. Secondly, by properly filing an UCC-1 Financing Statement we can become the holder in due course of the STRAWMAN. This gives us virtual ownership of the government created entity.

This is the power of contracts (commerce) and it should be mentioned, at least this one time, that a contract overrides the Constitution, the Bill of Rights, and any other document other than another contract. We should also mention that no process of law - "color" of law under present codes, statutes, rules, regulations, ordinances, etc. - can operate upon you, no agent and/or agency of government (including courts) can gain jurisdiction over you, WITHOUT YOUR CONSENT. You, (we) are not within their fictional commercial venue.

The Accepted for Value process, however, gives us the ability to deal with "them" through the use of our transmitting utility/go-between, the Strawman and hold them accountable in their own commercial world, for any action(s) they attempt to take against us. Without a proper Order, and now we know they're not in possession of such a document, they must leave us alone or pay the consequences.

Yes, this process IS powerful -- and one had better learn it well - should one choose to utilize it. My next book will go into detail about the entire accepted for value process and how to access your Treasury Deposit Account! Once you have completed this process you will be considered a Secured Party Creditor. This process cannot be used to make money, but it CAN set us free from government oppression and control.

SECURE PARTY CREDITOR

Now you may ask yourself the question what does becoming a Secure Party Creditor have to do with me? The answer to that question is becoming a Secure Party Creditor is your goal. Once completed, you will have established the foundation to manage the commercial affairs of the debtor, and the standing to protect yourself from all public claims made against your straw man (strawman), which is your name in ALL CAPITAL LETTERS. This can be accomplished by filing your UCC1 (UCC-1 Financing Statement).

While Secure Party Creditor status rebuts the presumption that you are property of the state, you must still bargain for your rights as a Sovereign. Only citizens (slaves) of the state have privileges. For Sovereigns, rights without contract are a fantasy.

The first step in returning yourself to a sovereign individual is that you have to take back your artificial straw man (strawman), and reclaiming it as YOUR debtor. If you were to take a look at your driver's license, social security card right now, you would see your name in all capital letters. That is your straw man (strawman) that the government created for you. In order to take back your straw man (strawman) you need to file a UCC-1 Financing Statement, filed with your Secretary of State's office. The UCC-1 defines exactly who the debtor is and who is the secured party creditor. Your name in all capital letters is the debtor and your name with initial capitals and the rest lower case letters, is you, the secured party creditor. As more and more people perform this process, some states are making the filing of UCC 1 forms more difficult, some states are refusing to file it all together.

The other part of the reclamation of your straw man (strawman) process is the Security Agreement. Though this document is not filed with the UCC-1 form, it should be referred to in the Financing Statement section of the UCC-1. It is a properly executed Security Agreement that makes your filing legitimate since it is an agreement between your flesh & blood you and your artificial you. You cannot go around making other people or entities your debtors unless you have something to back up your claim.

The UCC-1 form should be filed in your state of residence and state of birth since that is the 'port of entry' for your straw man (strawman). If you are living in and own property and/or do business in a different state at present, for your property protection, a UCC-1 should also be filed in your current state.

The Financing Statement as well as the other information filled in on the UCC-1 is most critical not only for the effectiveness of it, but also on the success in getting your forms filed. Prepare your UCC-1 Financial Agreement and your Security Agreement, Hold Harmless, Power of Attorney and Copyright documents.

How to Beat Debt Collectors

Forever!!!

In 2008 alone, over $123 billion in charged-off debts were sold to companies that then pursued those debts *as if they owned them*. They don't...at least not until you make a fatal mistake and give them the right. You see, when you signed the original agreement with your credit card company, <u>you signed a contract with your original credit card company</u>. Think about what I just said, because this is where winning your battle begins. Yes, you signed an agreement with your credit card company, but <u>you did not sign one with the companies that bought your debt</u> from the credit card company. Sound crazy? If they don't have a right to your debt, then why are they coming after you? Because you don't know your rights, they know this, and they collect billions of dollars every year at massive profits.

1.) <u>Defendant is without information or knowledge sufficient to form an opinion as to the truth or accuracy of Plaintiff's claim, and based on that denies generally and specifically Plaintiff's claim.</u>

This statement tells the court that you cannot claim to know whether or not this is actually your debt, because no proof of that ownership has been provided by the collection company, Plaintiff. Read, or quote, this statement, and add nothing further to what it says.

Now, a trick here is used when a plaintiff <u>does</u> show up in court in an attempt to trip you up and win through trickery alone. They will call you to the witness stand, brandish a copy of the original contract issued by the credit card company and ask you, under oath, if you are denying that you signed this agreement with the credit card company. <u>If you say that you are not denying that you signed the agreement, you lose</u>. You simply state that you are without knowledge sufficient to form an opinion as to the accuracy of the Plaintiff's claim, and add nothing more. You can repeat this as often as you need to until the judge loses his patience and orders the plaintiff to sit down. The plaintiff is waving a blank piece of paper in front of you. It does not contain your signature, and it is not the original signed agreement. It is worthless.

For your next step, you state the following:

2.) <u>Plaintiff has failed to state a claim upon which relief may be granted</u> -

Either no statute was cited, or the complaint fails to state facts sufficient to constitute a cause of action against you, the defendant. Listing the facts of the case may be enough to file a claim, but the plaintiff merely says the defendant owes the money, and this is not enough.

"Plaintiff's claim demands monies for an alleged debt for which no proof of said debt, nor proof of ownership of said debt, has been verified and exhibited." You want to state this.

3.) Defendant demands for proof of Plaintiff's ownership of alleged debt.

The law is very clear that the plaintiff has a legal duty to attach any necessary documentation to everything he has filed in court, including in the original certified letter that was sent to you. Did you see any documentation in that letter? No. Why? Because the plaintiff has none. He knows that, the court knows that, and now, you know that, too. Legally, the plaintiff lacks capacity to sue. At this point, you may read the following statement to the court:

"The plaintiff is required, by law, to trace in his statement of claim the derivation of his cause of action from his assignor so that the defendant may challenge the plaintiff's claim that he is the present owner of the cause of action."

What you just told the judge is that the plaintiff, in this case, the lawyer representing the collection company, has not presented proof that he, or his company, owns the debt. Why does he own it? Did you sign an agreement with him? Is he a credit card company? The answer is, no. You do not owe him, or his company, anything. He is required, by law, to show why you owe him, or his company. He will not be able to prove this...unless you have made one fatal mistake. If you have been scared into making any payment arrangements and have already made payments to his company, then I would seek legal help in unraveling their tentacles. Cardinal rule - do not make payments, or agreements to make payments, to any company that is calling about a debt that you owed someone else. Doing so creates a contract that may be binding.

As in most credit card cases (depending on your state), when a claim is "based upon a written agreement, the pleading shall state specifically if the agreement is oral or written." If the credit card claim is based upon a writing, then the plaintiff must "attach a copy of the writing." This means that, once again, the law requires that the plaintiff produce the original contract with the credit card company bearing your original signature. No blank contracts, no "supposed or forged" copies. The original, and only the original, will do.

Also, in most states, if the lawyer filing the claim for the collection company knowingly files a suit without having that original contract in hand, he is in violation of the law. He has to either have that contract, or he has to have someone with him coming to court who has personal knowledge of that signed contract, and he has neither. When he signed the suit papers, he stated that he had these proofs by his signature. A lawyer filing such a claim should be prosecuted, he deserves to be sued, and you can do so if you have a lawyer representing you.

Next, we come to:

4.) Insufficient specificity in a pleading.

When the lawyer for the collection company seeks damages based on a contractual relationship, an agreement or contract, and these damages are ascertainable based on that contract or agreement, then the lawyer is required to plead those damages with specificity. What this means is that the court is going to require that lawyer to include <u>facts</u> concerning <u>when you engaged in purchases that led to that debt</u>, <u>the amount of those purchases</u>, and <u>what those purchases were</u>. You can cite the following in court:

Citing Marine Bank, 25 Pa. D. & C.3d at 267-69. A "defendant is entitled to know the dates on which individual transactions were made, the amounts therefore and the items purchased to be able to answer intelligently and determine what items he can admit and what items he can contest."

Next on the list:

5.) <u>Defendant cites Failure of Consideration</u>:

"Whereas no exchange of money or goods occurred between the plaintiff and the defendant, therefore, defendant cites Failure of Consideration."

What you are saying here is that there was never any exchange of money or items of value between you and the collection company, between Plaintiff and Defendant. You tell the court that you never entered into any contractual or debtor/creditor arrangements with Plaintiff. Consideration is a necessary fact that the plaintiff is required to show in order to prove that you and the collection company had a valid, binding and enforceable agreement or contract. Consideration means that the collection company was giving you a service in exchange for your money. Were they a credit card company? Were they giving you credit? Not likely. Therefore, they were not giving you any "consideration," and you, therefore, do not have a contract with them.

Furthermore, the collection company would be required to show the terms of that agreement in court. Where is their contract with you? There is none. Because they cannot produce any such agreement or contract, this is "failure of consideration." They have no case, just one more reason they knew that they should not come to court, one more reason the judge is compelled to dismiss the case against you.

Next, we come to:

6.) Repudiation - Plaintiff is not named in any alleged agreement that is purported to have been entered into between Defendant and Plaintiff.

Here, you state that the plaintiff has not produced any contract between Defendant and (your collection company), naming Plaintiff as party to such contract. Defendant repudiates any claim to such a contract existing. As there was no "meeting of the minds," a necessary element of a valid contract, no contract exists. The plaintiff is not an assignee for the purported agreement, and the plaintiff has not produced any evidence that supports any related claims or assumptions. The lawyer for the collection company has failed to produce any document that shows that your original credit card company has named him, or his collection company, as assignees, nor has he even shown that the original credit card company has any knowledge of his actions, or that the original credit card company has even given this lawyer, or collection company, all rights and control.

If a credit card company did assign the debt to a third party, the creditor would then lose his rights to collect later. This means that your credit card company probably took a tax credit, an insurance write-off, or some such action that makes the credit card company unable to collect the debt after that point. They destroyed their records, and they moved on. The collection company does not have the original agreement with your signature, and they know that they have no case against you...unless you make the mistake of making an agreement with the collection company and then making a payment on it. Since there was no "meeting of the minds" between you and the collection company, a necessary element required to create a legal and binding contract between the two of you, their claim is repudiated.

If your original credit card company had made an agreement with the collection company, you were not a party to those terms. Just because an assignment clause exists in a credit agreement does not mean that it is sufficient to create a new obligation with the collection company. The assignment clause merely takes away the rights of your original credit card company to collect if they decide to assign it to another company, in this case the collection company. The collection company would then have to offer you a new contract, you would have to agree to its terms, and you would finally have to sign this new contract. If you have not signed a contract with the collection company, you owe them nothing.

In court, if you had to argue this, you would simply state that **Plaintiff is not an assignee for the purported agreement, and Plaintiff has not offered any evidence to the contrary. As there is no proof offered, assuming that it exists would create an unfair prejudice against the Defendant.**

Now, we move to:

7.) Defendant claims Lack of Privity as Defendant has never entered into any contractual or debtor/creditor arrangements with Plaintiff

You can simply state, **"Whereas no relationship exists between Plaintiff and Defendant, and whereas Defendant never signed a contract or agreement with Plaintiff, Defendant cites Lack of Privity."**

Privity is the legal term for a close, mutual, or successive relationship to the same right of property, or the power to enforce a promise or warranty. No relationship exists between the collection agency (Plaintiff) and Defendant. Defendant never signed a contract or agreement with the collection agency. A collection company cannot collect any amount of money that is not permitted by law or by agreement. Here is the law:

"It further states that the debt collector cannot collect any amount of money that is

not permitted by law or by the agreement.

Because there is no agreement between the collector and the alleged debtor, no collection can be sustained." (Fair Debt Collection Practices Act)

Nearing the end of our list, we come to:

8.) Plaintiff's complaint violates the Statute of Frauds

Plaintiff claims to have a contract with you, thus, Plaintiff has to produce it, because such a contract falls within a class of contracts or agreements required to be in writing. The purported contract or agreement alleged in the complaint was not in writing and signed by Defendant or by some other person authorized by Defendant and who was to answer for the debt, default, or miscarriage of another person. In order for the collection company to state that it had an agreement with you, it has to show how it was going to benefit you. For example, was the collection company going to issue you credit like a credit card company? Highly unlikely. Therefore, to say that it had a contract with you is fraudulent, because the collection company cannot provide the same services as the credit card company did. It would be like the credit card company selling your contract to another company that required you to sell your house to them at the end of one year. This new requirement would not be something that you agreed to in the original contract, and since there was no "meeting of the minds," you did not come to any agreement with the collection company. Here, then, you simply cite **statute of frauds**. Research your state's case law to see how your state stands on this point. Nonetheless, because the collection company cannot provide the same services as the original credit card company, it is breach of contract, thus, we invoke "statute of frauds."

Lastly, we come to:

9.) **Scienti et volenti non fit injuria** - "An injury is not done to one who knows and wills it."

The laws in this country do not provide a remedy for a collection company that knowingly and voluntarily takes on a bad debt and then goes after the debtor in an attempt to collect that alleged debt. What the law says is that an entity cannot place itself in harm's way and then sue for damages. Thus, "scienti et volenti non fit injuria." That would be like you standing in front of a speeding car, then suing the driver for damages. You put yourself in harm's way, you deserve no damages. The collection company bought a debt that was bad, then wanted it paid. Just cite scienti et volenti non fit injuria, and the judge will know what you mean.

Most collection companies know not to go after debts that are past the statute of limitations, but, there are still those who do, so you should know that most states will not allow claims on debts that are more than three years old. In some states, that statute of limitations is four years. You want to research this so that you know what your state allows, because the collection company pursuing you may have waited too long, and you may just have a right to have the suit thrown out on this technicality alone.

As I stated earlier, quite often, the credit card company has made an insurance claim, or taken a tax deduction, and this is known as accord and satisfaction. This renders the debt satisfied and legally, no one can attempt any further to collect this debt. Your collection company knows this, yet they are still trying to take you to court, because they know that if you do not show up, the law then reverses everything, and you end up owing them. So, go to court. Just the fact that you file an intent to defend yourself lets them know that you are aware of your rights, that their best bet is to call off the bluff, and that they should go find some other person to try to fool into entering a contract with them for a debt that is otherwise uncollectible.

Remember that the Fair Debt Collection Practices Act requires all debt collectors to validate the collection upon request of the purported debtor. The collection company will not be able to, so, stand your ground with everything that I have written in this article. They deserve to lose, because they know they are acting illegally, yet they use all kinds of trickery and deceit to win. You can fight back by simply using the law and your legal rights.

Make sure that you check every rule that I have quoted to make sure that there are not any deviations in your state. State laws will vary, and State laws vary from Federal laws, so do your homework.

This book is intended to give you back the knowledge that was intentionally hidden from you. Now that you have read this, you can understand the reason why they have NEVER taught us this in school. If "the powers that be" had to deal with people who were woke, then their power and control over us would be greatly diminished! So, I implore you to continue to do your research and use this as a starting point for freeing yourself and your mind. I appreciate that you have taken the time to read this and I encourage you (if you have got anything at all out of this) to share it with someone who you feel my benefit from this information. Again, this is not my opinion, this is a compilation of research that has taken me years to compile and understand. God bless, and have a great time on your journey to the next level in educating yourself!

Made in the USA
Columbia, SC
06 May 2019